RockStars

Growing Stellar Performers in Organizations

Rozaine Cooray and Pujitha Silva

First Print – 2018

RockStars

Growing Stellar Performers in Organizations

ISBN: 9781717737106
Imprint: Independently published

Published by, Rozaine Cooray and Pujitha Silva

ALSO BY ROZAINE COORAY

FROM CRISIS TO CHARACTER, 2014

A COLLECTION OF PUBLISHED ARTICLES BASED ON ORGANIZATIONAL PSYCHOLOGY ON HOW TO NAVIGATE DAY-TO-DAY CHALLENGES AT WORK

COLOURS OF THE SUN, 2010

A NOVEL. SHORTLISTED FOR GRATIAEN AWARDS AND STATE LITERARY AWARDS, 2010

For Yavin

Dedications

Writing is my first love and being able to find time to write amidst many other roles I play is a privilege. RockStars happened to be something I initially saw myself being forced into, when Pujitha mentioned the importance of making the P3 GROWTHS Model available for many to critique, appreciate and apply in their own lives. We had worked on the research and ideas for the book for over three years and we were well into the sixth draft. It had been read and evaluated by our team many a time. Yet the writer in me was not convinced. It was as if something was missing.

I have much to be grateful for, for the walks on the beach which largely gave me the inspiration at the time to work its magic. It brought together different people, stories and perspectives to crystallize some specific anecdotes that fitted well to the stages of the Model. In the quest of searching for the missing piece of the story, one morning it occurred to me the importance of keeping it simple. And just like that, it came together; the P3 GROWTHS Model, Pujitha's work on the human body as a leadership model for over 10 years, the research done by our teams and now the plot of the story.

The story line of this book came together during a course of one day while spending time with my then one-year old son. The journey of the book in many ways resembled some of the junctures in our own paths. Writing this book, challenged me to address my own biases to truly step up to change the way I looked at a situation. Some chapters took longer than others but the higher the stage in the model, the more challenging it was for me to write without sounding preachy.

I want to acknowledge my support system that made this book possible. I want to thank our team at Forté Consultancy and Full Life Coaching, especially Kartini and Raiha, who worked on the research aspect of human behaviour at each stage. I want to thank our parents, who continue to believe in us and support us even when they fail to understand why we do what we do. Finally, I want to thank our Chairman, the wonderful father he is for us, for believing in us and mentoring us to achieve our goals.

As a Psychologist, RockStars provided me a platform to understand human behaviour (myself included) at each level of the Model. And as a writer, it helped me to realize the importance of simplicity and timing. As a wife, it encouraged me to focus on the synergy of our strengths and as a mother, RockStars gave me the hope to work in creating a better world for our children.

Rozaine Cooray

From the Author of the P3 GROWTHS Model

What is life all about? How can one find fulfillment in life? These were thoughts and ideas that I grappled with for some years. I struggled to understand how we could all uniquely contribute to the world, and how we could wholeheartedly pursue this mission without being tied down by the strappings of life.

Most of us are happy in our comfort zones, and life needs to give us a rude awakening to pull us out of these comfort zones to pursue what is meaningful to us. More often than not, we tend to stay in the mundane, because we lack courage, or due to the excuses we give ourselves, waiting for that perfect moment, to step into the unknown.

For a new life to begin, there needs to be a death. Not necessarily the death of a person but a death to an old way of doing things, an old habit, a form or structure that has kept us hardwired in the status quo of life.

My world was shaken in 2004 during the Tsunami, when I saw much death and destruction around me, but that was not strong enough to draw me out of my comfort zone. Then in 2008, my father had a stroke. Watching life ebbing away from a once healthy person who was dear to me was the beginning of an awakening. In 2009, I lost my job as a design engineer in Australia, during the global financial crisis, signaling the death to yet another phase in my life. This released me to explore new opportunities towards a life of greater meaning and purpose. Eventually, when in 2011 my dad passed away, I felt the shift within me to start serious change. It was now or never.

I began to explore the idea of life's purpose, and how one's mission and accomplishments in life could be passed down to another generation in a way that life and success would continue past our time, so that the next generation may live a better life. This reignited and reinforced a passion for mentoring and coaching, which I knew would be a way of life for me and the birthing of a new professional identity as a Life and Executive Coach.

I was led to try and integrate the different facets of my life to create one fulfilled life, which for me, was the beginning of a new journey of growth. The engineer in me tried to understand how exactly this would be propagated. From my background in Biomedical Engineering, I knew how the human body is a complex system of integrated structures, organized in a systematic way where cells form tissues, tissues form organs, organs form systems, to eventually form the body, whilst all sharing a common DNA. I was led to consider whether the lessons on how the human body is organized could be used to transform the organizations we are a part of, the families, companies, cities, societies, and even countries. The engineer in me also tried to bring a sense of process, orderliness and structure to this idea of growth and how it is brought about. These ideas came together to form the P3 GROWTHS Model (Figure 01).

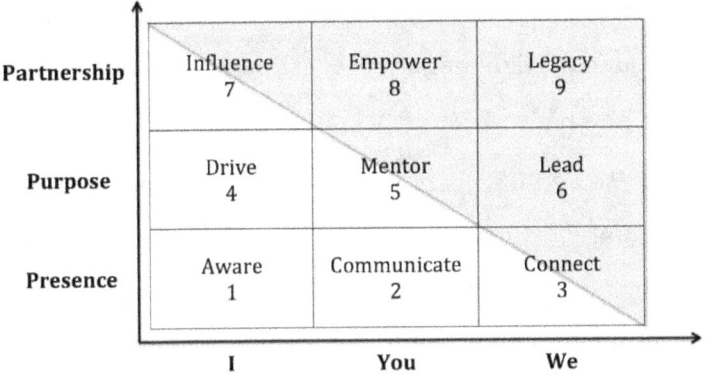

Figure 01. P3 GROWTHS Model

The P3 GROWTHS Model describes growth as a combined response of 3 stages, namely Presence, Purpose and Partnership in facilitating meaningful change. Presence is about making a connection or perceiving the change required. Purpose helps shape the direction of the intended change. Partnership leads to taking action towards making the change a reality. The model explores the idea that growth occurs in 3 areas, in relation to the 'I' (intrapersonal), 'YOU' (interpersonal), and 'WE' (community). These concepts are captured in the nine-stage model of growth, and each individual stage will be elaborated on in the chapters that follow.

Yet, despite the model having come to life, I lacked the confidence and courage to explore how the model could be applied, tested and developed further to fit into a corporate setting. It was at this juncture that I met Rozaine Cooray, a Psychologist practicing in organizations in Sri Lanka, working towards building people and organizations. With her insights and encouragement, I was able to better see how the model could be applied to the different facets of organizational life.

Together, over the next few years, we explored the model's application in transforming corporate organizations, and sectors such as education, and overall communities. Programs were developed and facilitated; our work was presented at international conferences and published in journals. However, there was a need to share the model in a simpler way such that a wider audience could learn from it. This led to the writing of RockStars: a book that could be read by people from different stages and walks of life, to share the lessons of the model in a personally meaningful way.

RockStars brings to you, the P3 GROWTHS Model, woven into a story line by Rozaine, with the intention of creating awareness in you towards a paradigm of growth and success that can ultimately lead to a fulfilled life. It brings to you the stories of real people that we met on our journey, who believed and embodied the principles of growth and transformation that the P3 GROWTHS Model stands for. The book is a presentation of struggles, the pains of change, and the stepping stones in life that lead to finding fulfillment.

The journey of bringing this book to life has truly tested us. We had to experience death in many ways, to old dreams we could have pursued, of success we commonly see being defined by society and culture, in light of the greater vision of transforming the society we live in, and of creating a better life for the next generation. The journey has transformed us and given us greater meaning and purpose, as I hope it will for you too.

Dr. Pujitha Silva

Foreword

Amidst many books on leadership and personal development, *RockStars* stands out with the simplicity of the ideas it offers. Written by Rozaine and Pujitha, two individuals who are passionate about transforming lives and communities, *RockStars* is a book that conveys the truths of life and leadership in a unique way.

In *RockStars,* Rozaine and Pujitha have conveyed ideas about transformation through the conversations between two men who sit at two points of their middle-age years. The characters are relatable; real people with flaws and who have gone through struggles. Insights and pearls of wisdom about life are intertwined into the characters' stories and in the resolution of their struggles. What is most unique is the use of organs from the human body as an analogy and source of lessons on the truths of leadership, strength, and life.

RockStars highlights and emphasizes a concept of yesteryears that became outdated - role modelling. It reminds us the importance of role models in nurturing good values in individuals. After all, in the early years of human civilization, dynasties were built and knowledge was shared, purely through the transfer of wisdom from father to son – from generation to generation.

Over the years, people shifted to sharing and accessing information through the written word. As the "gurus" and "experts" started conveying messages tinged with hidden agendas and conflicts of interest, a need arose for unbiased sources of information. Thus, scholarly articles and scientific reviews became the primary mode of knowledge sharing and learning. With RockStars, we are encouraged to find role models and gurus who are of good character, who drive no hidden agendas. It inspires us to seek these individuals to find the lessons and insights that cannot be found in scholarly articles, but are only found in real stories of real people.

RockStars carries in its pages, stories of vulnerability, of authenticity, of the importance of character and values, in running the race to success. It calls the reader to pause and reflect on who we are, what we do, and why we do it. It shifts our focus from achieving too much too soon; to focus on achieving what is *actually* meaningful.

As a doctor and an educator, I see *RockStars* bringing change and transformation in lives by forcing us to ask the questions we stopped answering, urging us to learn from the past that can nourish us for the future, by reminding us that in the 'rat-race' to success, we have the responsibility of preserving our integrity and being good people.

It was my pleasure reading *RockStars,* and believe that the next reader will find this book not only insightful in the context of life, but also entertaining and heart-warming in the story it narrates.

To Rozaine and Pujitha, I offer my best wishes for the success of this book, and hope that this is the next step in creating the transformation they envision in families, organizations, and the country as a whole.

Dr. Rukshan C Fernandopulle

MBBS, MS, MRCOG (UK), MRCP (Ireland)

Consultant Obstetrician & Gynaecologist

Senior Lecturer in Obstetrics & Gynaecology

University of Sri-Jayawardenapura

Eye for thy light

Ear for thy words

Hand for thy grasp

Heart for thy pulse

Spine for thy form

Brain for thy thought

Mouth for thy pitch

Air for thy lungs

Womb for thy child

Blood for thy life

Oh! The perfection of thy human body

And the imperfection in thee!

At work

Just a week ago, I didn't know what I was signing up for when I had that crucial conversation on my performance feedback with the new Managing Director. My feedback had been excellent as always; what else can you expect from a fiercely ambitious manager who has diligently mastered the art of his functional unit over the years? I am known to be a good manager, approachable, open- minded and friendly, but also focused and serious about delivery. Mainly, my job has been to make decisions, give guidance, train people on their tasks and manage the overall operations, and 'operations' is what I am good at. Being an engineer by profession, I have always worked with systems and processes, and numbers and analyses are what I am comfortable with.

Six months ago, my former boss had opted for an early retirement due to his deteriorating health. A workaholic himself, this realization that he may have spent too much time at office under tremendous stress over the years, had occurred far too late. The team and I dearly miss him but we are also thankfully relieved that he had invested much in our growth so that we have been able to operate without a boss till now.

Today, when the MD asks me whether I happen to have any concerns, I don't hesitate to be honest about the boredom that is setting in. I am thirty-five years old, and have faithfully served this company for twelve years now and it has been my home since I joined the workforce as a management trainee. My former boss had been talking to me about setting up the operations in a new plant that is coming up in the vicinity and the possible vacancy as the Factory Manager. He had told me that I topped the list in the succession plan, so last year was all about training and coaching for this unannounced position. I knew that there were others who were more experienced than me and that such a promotion would be a contentious one. However, I was willing to take up the challenge as this role would finally validate why I had worked so hard all these years and stayed with the company, despite having had opportunities to join other companies which probably were better paymasters.

Honestly apart from having the two kids, career-wise, life has not been very challenging in the last five years. Of course I have had transfers from one plant to another to train and ensure quality and productivity, and to initiate new processes and have new systems up and running. However, the satisfaction has been somewhat short-lived. My growth within the company has been mostly horizontal – acquiring different variations of the same skill. What I now want is something more, even though I don't know how to articulate what I want. The new MD (who I hear is from the US and a trusted friend of the owners of the company) seems to be a task-master. During our initial chat, he asks me whether I am willing to take up a different task but doesn't make any mention of the position that I have been trained for.

He mentions that he is not happy, in fact disturbed by the rate of turnover and absenteeism amongst the machine operators, a phenomenon that has been constantly high for many, many years.

This is an industry trend, and I hope he is aware of it.

He describes how internal research based on exit interviews and community research externalized the reasons, attributing it to new mushrooming factories in the neighborhood offering better incentives.

I mention to him the personal and social issues faced by our female workers, and how we have over the years provided them with support and empowered them as much as we could, to which he responds, 'Now, this is all true. Except that it is not the total picture'.

He emphatically mentions that the internal research maybe biased, that it fails to see the loopholes within our own system; he adds that we need to have a better emotional working environment.

'People think it's just about the incentives. There's more, there's definitely more to what meets the eye. People leave their bosses Roy, not necessarily the company. And I am sure there are other reasons and we need to get to the root of the problem to see why people are leaving at this rate. I don't think we are inhuman; in fact we have some of the best CSR initiatives in the country. However, we may be mechanical in how we relate to our people or make them feel. We have to get off our high horses and connect with them at their level. This is why our corporate office and the high end executives can be very unpopular amongst them. This is your model factory. You change this factory and give us the recipe to replicate it in other factories too', he says.

Eh! Hold on! Isn't it...

'Look, I want to get it done. We have to address this. I want to put you in charge of a change initiative that involves all the line managers and supervisors of the machine operators. One, I want to see how the workers feel about their supervisors, one by one, with all the names included. Two, I want you to give these managers feedback the way you think is right. You make a call on that. Three, I want you to tell them that they have six months to change and that we will support them in whatever way possible. At the end of six months, we would carry out this study again and if they have failed to change by then, we will have to let them go. I want to make this factory great. That's why I have been hired and you are my man for this, Roy'.

I stare at him, completely startled by his request; in my opinion, it is lopsided. We, as a company, are doing really well, so why upset the apple cart? We hit the numbers even before the stipulated timelines and our managers have endured and served the company during tough times. How arrogant of him to think that his initiative would change anything for the better.

If at all, it'll be disastrous. Who the hell hired this guy?! And hey, listen. The engineer in me likes to keep the talking to a minimum and focus on what needs to be done, step by step, systematically. I am not comfortable with listening to how people 'feel'; as wrong as it may sound, that is the truth. I think people should come to work in order to work. Feelings are for family and home.

I am lost in a whirlwind of thoughts.

'I have observed you Roy,' he continues. 'I think you are the right person; you have the right temperament. You have so far not offended anyone. Everyone likes you and you are good at what you do. You have credibility because you know what you are talking about'.

'Not when it comes to this', I tell him still horrified by the thought of it. 'I am clueless'.

'You'll learn the ropes around this job. Just a heads up. It's going to be tough, so be prepared to be the bad guy. I am sure now, we will be able to talk about your real growth in six months. Make me proud and moreover, make yourself proud', he adds encouragingly.

What? I am flabbergasted. This is not the offer I have been expecting. This offer seems to be that of an underdog's, leaving me speechless and somewhat paralyzed from the neck downwards. Maybe there is a hidden agenda. Maybe this guy is setting me up for failure so if we didn't perform as a team, he could blame it on me. Why should I even trust this man? Maybe I should speak to the cluster CEO or GM. But by doing that, will I breach the pecking order? Shock mode on; my mind is a tornado of questions and indignations.

The company has invested on expensive executive training programs for the top performers and I have been sent on some of the most prestigious ones so to speak. This is payback time, yes, but hey! Can some new guy order me around like this to fire people if it comes to that? Am I not too young for this role to begin with? How would most of the senior management respond to this?

'I need to grab something to eat before my next meeting; it's the management meeting and I will tell the board that I have put you in charge. This is coming from the top Roy - the 'very top'; first priority of the quarter. We will announce the role tomorrow to the factory. It is a double promotion in my opinion, 'Head of Change Management' and you would directly report to me. If you are wondering what HR would say about it- they already know, and they think that it is better that a separate unit handles it'.

'The very top, meaning the "founders"?' I ask.

'Yes, I was specifically asked to come from the US to see that things are done differently. I was an engineer myself there working for Ford', he explains.

'I don't know. This is definitely beyond the scope of what I can offer to this company. I know nothing about change management. Besides, I was trained to oversee the operations of the new plant', I say, overwhelmed.

My wife usually tells me I am painfully calm even when I am supposed to be emotionally charged, when people cross the boundaries. But not today, not after hearing this.

'That's why you'd have to learn then. All the best Roy. This is an offer based on potential and trust; so congratulations'. With a brief nod in my direction, we shake hands and part.

A perfect storm!

....

I wake up to the sound of the alarm, loud and shrill next to my ear. Sighing, I sit up in bed. I look out through the glass window, and gaze for a few seconds at the stars in the sky. The alarm reads 4.30 a.m. It is time for my morning run. Our natural alarm clock is fast asleep in his cradle, today. He had turned five months just yesterday.

I have long since been trying to get into the habit of going for a run every morning, and of course with the excuses I make to stay in bed a bit longer, exercise seems to be the last thing on my list. Living just minutes' walk from the beach, I am at an advantage. Nevertheless, I have taken a while to get accustomed to waking up earlier again after the birth of our son. But today, I have no choice, and as I absorb the first moments of wakefulness, my thoughts enter a world of turmoil, turmoil that still flusters me in my sleep. How am I going to approach this new role? Why did I ask for more challenge? There is no one but me to blame.

I stealthily rush downstairs not wanting to wake my wife up. I skim through yesterday's papers while waiting for the water to boil for my coffee. An article in the bottom corner of the paper catches my eye. It isn't the contents of the article on reforms of a chain of companies in the country that interests me, but the salt and pepper haired man in the photo who looks achingly familiar. The article goes to say how this medical doctor (who had been practicing in the UK) turned Vice President of a chain of companies employing sixty-thousand people, has gone on to transform the business in a bottom up approach, saving the organization from a massive bankruptcy in its core business units.

I continue to read more about this doctor and his team as I sip my coffee. Then it dawns on me who he is: the guy who walks at lightning speed on the beach with a stick in his hand to chase off stray dogs who might occasionally cross his path. Ah! That's right! Never knew he is a medical doctor.

The article interests me particularly, because of the dilemma I have regarding my own work situation. I put the paper away, check my earphones and leave the house hoping the run will help me to get some clarity in my thinking.

I cross the rail tracks, and walk out onto the beach. I glance around for a few seconds, before plugging in my earphones and starting to jog, in the direction of the Mount Lavinia Hotel. I jog to the beat pounding loudly in my ears. Each time I feel tired, I slow down to a brisk walk. In this manner, I reach the end of the beach strip, right next to the hotel. At this place, I pause for a while to look around. I take in the mild light of early dawn, as the gentle breeze soothes the aching muscles, when I suddenly notice the familiar face from the papers walking by. 'Aha! I knew I've seen this guy before', I think to myself while appraising the tall, slender man who seems to be in his mid-to-late fifties; Oh well! It's difficult to guess.

I smile and nod a greeting, and he salutes me in response.

'That's an incredible story, to turn something around like that', I call out as he passes me heading back in the same direction.

'Ah! Yes. I like to stay away from the limelight. Don't enjoy it much you see', he says still walking.

'Yeah I know what you mean', I add wanting to join him in conversation.

'Boy, you got to walk faster than that if we are going to chat,' he says laughingly. 'The old man needs his exercises'. He extends his hand and introduces himself, 'I am Edward but you can call me Ed.'

'And I am Roy', I respond with a handshake.

'I hear you were a doctor before. That's interesting; doctor to a Vice President in the corporate world. You must be someone who loves change', I comment.

He smiles, 'Change is inevitable when you take the macro view. So, it's not about whether you like it or not; it's about whether you can take it or not'.

He grins and asks me about my family, and draws some reference to his wife who is from the area being friends with someone we know in common. He asks me about my wife, kids and work. When it comes to the topic of my work, I struggle to answer in confidence.

'I go as Head of Operations at the moment, but there's a bit of change that's taking place within the company; so I think my role will change in the days to come which makes everything uncertain at this stage', I reply hesitantly.

'And you are someone who hates change?' he asks, smiling knowingly.

I nod bashfully. 'Yeah somewhat, but it depends on the area; I am ok with machines and people who can fit into a system; you know, the things that can be planned and organized'.

'You mean you like predictability and to be in control of a situation. Do you think the sense of control comes with the system in place?' he asks.

'Hmmm...you could say that', I add. 'It's more about the touchy feely stuff that I am uncomfortable with. That's definitely not my area', I smile.

'Ah! I understand', he says looking across the shore. 'Look, I got to stop here as that small shop across the railway lines has the meanest toast bread, dahl curry and sambol. You are welcome to join me if you like', he offers invitingly.

I feel slightly disappointed as I remember that I have promised my team to meet them over breakfast at the factory an hour before work, which meant leaving to work early.

'I'll definitely join you next time but for today I need to head to work pretty early. Maybe I can meet you Saturday morning?', I ask hoping he'd say yes.

'Yeah, sure. But I don't run like you. I walk. So if you are okay to walk, we can meet on Saturday', he says with a wave of his hand as he heads towards the rail tracks.

'I'll walk with you sir', I tell him, relieved that I'd get another chance to meet this guy.

For some reason, I feel a sense of hope as if this guy may have the answers I am looking for.

As I run back towards home, a good thirty minute run, I am surprised by my own openness with the guy. I rarely talk about work with anyone. Desperate, I am! I think. But hey! What a difference a day makes!

....

Back at work

During the week at work, I find out that the management would put a hold on the announcement of the new promotion, till I get my homework done on how to initiate this project. I am to present my plan next week to my boss.

My boss has told me that I should do this alone as the findings will be very sensitive. What I do not anticipate is the reluctance to co-operate from some of the crucial people from HR. This promotion where I would function as an independent party in an area that overlaps with that of HR, is being seen as unacceptable and downright insulting for some in the team, including some Senior Managers. I can really do without this drama but the gauntlet is thrown, and there is no going back.

I try to see who can really help me in this, who will be on my side. I put down flowcharts, and request some statistics from HR to be made available to me. On top of my current role that I still have to fulfill, I find myself overly absorbed in the how, what and why of the whole initiative. I like to believe that people would be on my side, that they would cooperate, collaborate and combine forces with me.

In my frustration, I reach out to speak to one of my good friends outside of work and he suggests how it looks like, that I am the pawn that the company would now manipulate to get the unpleasant work done, to spell out what they don't want to, to fire the people they don't have the courage to confront. Speaking to him does not help at all, and with the increasing amount of chores in the home front after the second baby, my stress and the lack of sensitivity towards household issues, is not really welcomed by my wife either.

The following week is a horror. I find myself thinking even in my sleep: putting models and processes together in order to plan it out, keeping the repercussions in mind. I get occasionally disturbed by the impending deadlines.

I feel overly cautious and aware of the emotions slowly simmering around the factory, because despite claims of confidentiality, someone has (as always) leaked the secret. I find myself having to explain to people why this change is underway, justifying why it is I who will be driving this change. I receive countless text messages, emails from personal email addresses, and many perplexed looks from faces in the cafeteria. My conversations with peers become non-personal, overly technical, and almost fake. I become extremely sensitive to the passive-aggression around that is brewing somewhat strongly beneath the surface.

One morning, Naren, my colleague, whom I have been grooming to take on my position in Operations, approaches me in the cafeteria, and says 'Roy, I know this is hard for you. I know what people are thinking and how difficult it maybe for you to ignore it, but know that I am there to support you. Apart from making sure that everything in Operations flows smoothly, I can make time after work to support you in anything you need me to do'.

He further adds laughingly, 'When the going gets tough, the tough get going'.

I smile, thank him, and ask him to oversee the Operations unit for the time being.

....

EYE FOR THY LIGHT

Back at home in the night, my wife often finds me awake whenever she wakes up to nurse the baby in the early hours of the morning, and then there are other times I pretend to be asleep. There are also instances when the need to get things off my chest is too strong, that I relate the happenings of the day and my plans on how I could approach this initiative. Most of the time, she looks at me nonplussed but listens patiently. She would always finish off the conversation with a reminder that I am prone to high cholesterol and blood pressure (as a result of generational garbage) during times of high stress. In one instance, she went on to suggest that maybe I should speak to a few friends from outside work or even get the help of a consultant who could assist me in planning it out.

The plus side of this insomnia is that I am able to get my exercise done. I remain sleepless in bed till 4.30 am, then have my coffee, and go on to run the whole length of the beach, which helps me clear my thoughts. It has been five days since my first chat with Ed, and as agreed I am waiting by the railway tracks, when I see Ed walking towards me, illuminating his path on the dark street with a flashlight.

'Good morning Ed!' I call out expectantly.

'A very good morning!' he replies as he switches off the torch.

Once again, I am struck by how energetic he is –a delightful trait to see. I envy his bursts of positive energy.

'So you told me Roy, that there's a lot of uncertainty in your job?' asks Ed after casual chitchat about current politics in the country. I am cautious about who I divulge information to about my company.

'Ah Ed, I have too many questions which I cannot put into words. In a nutshell, I'm trying to wrap my head around a new initiative the company wants me to lead in an area that I have very little idea of. I actually don't know from where to start', I respond, honestly confused about what to ask. 'But to start with, maybe you can tell me what you think is the most important thing in the life of a professional?', I ask, hoping that this general question would open up many discussion points.

'Ah! You think I'm a guru!', he laughs. 'I'm not, Roy. I can only tell you what I've learnt in my life.'

He continues, 'To answer your question, the most important thing in life is to see beyond the prison of our own thinking. Let me start with a story'.

'Once, there were two criminals who were on a life-sentence in two adjacent cells, in one of the most notorious prisons. Everyday, one of the prisoners would relate stories about the happenings on the playground of a school that was next to this prison', he narrates.

'Through his small window, he would look and share stories about different children and the games they played. He would specify the actions of children in so much detail that he had stories that would fill in the first half of the day. Next to the school was a market-place, and during weekends, he would relate the happenings within each stall – from fresh produce, to the dairies' and the butchers', he continues.

'Years went by, till one day, the stories all stopped. The prisoner had died late in the night, and his body had been removed before the other prisoner had a chance to pay his last respects. They had never seen each other given the strict rules that applied within the compound', Ed pauses for a few moments.

He continues, 'However, the other prisoner asks the guards whether he could have the cell of his friend, the one with a small window. The guard looks at him and exclaims "what window?"' he stops and pauses.

'"Well, the window through which the other prisoner would look outside to narrate stories about the children in the playground and the market place", he responds. Then the guard replies, "Ah! That would not have been possible even if he had a window"' he stops again to look at the horizon before he speaks.

' The guard said, "Not only was the cell completely sealed but he was also completely blind".'

I feel the goose-bumps rise on my skin.

'Wow' I utter.

We walk for a while in silence.

'The real sight is "insight". With our eyes intact, we could still be blind'. Ed completes the story.

We walk in silence. The mornings are slightly chilly in November and I notice how the sea has carved its territory differently this morning on the beach. The high dunes have been lowered and new ridges are being formed to accommodate the strong currents of the waves.

Ed speaks, 'Roy tell me, what is the most important part of a house or a building?'

'The foundation', I answer.

'Yes, you are right, because it is the base on which everything else is built'. Ed agrees and continues to walk.

"I am going to share a personal story with you. When we were schooling, during big matches in one of our somewhat junior years, my friends and I experimented with alcohol. You know what it is like to be in an adolescent peer group wanting to grow up too fast. It didn't agree with me much, and I spent three days sick in bed, obviously not the best first experience'.

I smile at Ed, picturing the scene.

He continues, 'My mother got me to promise her that I would never try it again until I was out of school. Believe it or not, I kept my promise. In the more senior years, no one could really persuade me to drink as I was resolute and strong. This continued during my university years and it was tough for anyone to challenge me to enjoy even a glass of wine'.

'Almost seven years since my promise to my mother, I met this beautiful girl at a party through my friends', Ed relates with a wide grin. 'I was so completely blinded by her that when she offered me a drink, I just didn't want to say no; maybe at the time I thought that she would think I was weak if I did so. All went well until it was time for us to go home and then there is this movie-like customary brawl over the girl. How predictable right? And guess who the superman in love was? And a drunken one for that matter', he says laughingly.

'So I beat some people up in a very uncharacteristic rescue mission. I got jailed for half a day until mother dearest had to come along and rescue me; you can imagine the shame! She told me that day "Well Ed, I got you to promise me not to try it till you are out of school. Now that you are in Medical College, it is your choice. But now, I have another request to make. Please do not ever, ever do anything that is not 'YOU' just to please someone or to fit in. I thought I have taught you better". And then, my mum who had never ever raised her hand to me, slapped me hard right there at the police station saying. "This is for being a total idiot'", Ed smiles reminiscently.

'You know Roy, that memory still remains one of the most vivid incidents, and even though it has been years since she passed away, I consider her to be the one that laid the foundation. When she was on her deathbed, as not so long after that incident she developed a rare brain condition, she told me that who I am is my greatest gift for the world, and that I need to strengthen what I am good at while being aware of my limitations', Ed pauses, gazing at the horizon with emotion.

'She told me this beautiful story of two men at a wood-chopping contest, one giant and one dwarf who competed against each other to judge who would chop the most amount of wood by the end of the day. The giant laughed at the sight of the dwarf and humiliated him for even considering contesting side by side with him. During the competition, the giant noticed the dwarf leaving to take a short break every two hours or so. The giant would laugh and insult his competitor saying, "Being short is bad enough; now you even take breaks. How do you suppose you could beat me?", to which the dwarf would keep quiet' Ed relates.

'At the end of the contest, when it was time to count the number of logs chopped, the giant was surprised to find out that the dwarf had chopped more wood. He asked the dwarf, "How did you manage to do that?" The dwarf, unperturbed, answered, "You thought I was taking a break every two hours. I was merely leaving to sharpen my axe"', he concludes.

I smile at how Ed drives the message here through his stories, almost transporting me to my younger years.

Ed continues, 'Seems like a childhood fable, but she narrated this when I was well into my twenties. You see Roy, this story helped me not only to realize my strengths, but also to continue sharpening them in the years to come, and this became an integral part of my identity'.

'She told me I could choose to define myself as a doctor, a son, a man, or whoever I saw myself as. She said that first and foremost, I am me, and that I should never compromise on that identity, what I hold dear, because deviating from it would mean cutting corners on my values' he says.

'She told me, "See, the dwarf was never shamed of who he was; he was never overconfident about his skill, nor did he falter when others unreasonably humiliated him. He was sure about himself, because he knew who he was". This served me well over the years, Roy'.

Ed pauses for a few moments.

'OK, so how would you define this identity?' I ask.

'Those are the foundational stones. The ones that are hardest to break'.

'Like?'

'Values, principles, morals. I mean whatever you want to call it but what continues to dominate your decisions and actions. Almost acting as DNA for behavior at times', Ed explains.

We walk a few more meters in silence.

'Roy, what do you see?', Ed asks, suddenly.

'You mean what I see now?', I ask him.

'Yes', he replies.

'I can barely see much except the far-away buildings under the patches of brightness, thanks to the glowing road lights. It's still quite dark', I answer.

'Roy, I want you to observe; can you not see anything? I know that it is a dark morning and there is little moonlight, but can you not see anything at all? Not even my silhouette tagging alongside yours?' he challenges.

Feeling slightly embarrassed, I answer, 'Oh! I see you, I see the white effervescence of the waves, I see the sky slightly turning colour from pitch dark to being just dark, the stars, and I see the lights of the hotel...'

I continue till Ed interrupts, 'Okay, if you are to see everything as they are, what would you need?'

This sure sounds like a viva. 'Light, we need light to see', I reply unsure about how he would respond.

'Ah ha! Light', Ed says.

Ed stops as if to absorb the sound of the waves breaking into the shore. We walk for a minute or two in silence. Then as a giant wave approaches the small stony pier crashing with a loud roar, Ed adds, 'Light is an incredible energy'.

I notice the change of colour in the eastern sky. The sky is a dark purple blue turning almost into a thick layer of navy blue. The sea in return is lighting up as the spray covers us from head to toe. I remove my glasses to clean them with my t-shirt.

'How do we see Roy?', Ed suddenly disturbs the silence waking me up from my contemplation.

'With our eyes of course?', I answer, and add again, 'I mean first with our eyes, then with the other senses'.

Ed continues with his explanation.

'The eye is a remarkable organ: it is one of the powerful doorways to the world around us. It is complex and it enables us to perceive the colour, shape, depth, and motion of objects in our surroundings by taking in light. The retina, like the film in a camera initiates a message to the brain about the image of the visual world'.

He pauses for a while to stretch his arms in front of him. I look ahead at the great Indian Ocean, and watch the waves for a while. We start walking again quietly for some time.

'Visible light is electromagnetic radiation that is visible to the human eye, and is responsible for the sense of sight. This is what we commonly call "light". This is only a small fraction of the entire electromagnetic spectrum. There are other types of radiation that we cannot see. What we physically see is what we sense, and what we sense is what shapes our perceptions about ourselves and the world', he explains.

Ed continues, 'We cannot see or appreciate most of the electromagnetic field, but that does not mean they cease to exist around us. Just the way our eyes perceive only certain frequencies of electromagnetic radiation, we as humans are also only aware of certain things in our surroundings.

We are literally blind to so much that is around us! To add to that, we filter through what we see in life, choosing to focus on some things and not on others; often overlooking perspectives different or contradictory to ours'.

'To be aware is to open the inward eye, to recognize ourselves, first and foremost', Ed explains. 'For this, we not only need reflection, but feedback from others and openness to new experiences and learning. We need flexibility in thinking and action. This not only helps to gain more awareness of ourselves, but also of the situation and others around us'.

I add with the little knowledge I have, 'And the blind spots we have are just like the blind spot in the retina that "fails to see"'.

'Ah! Yes!', Ed agrees happily.

He pauses for a while, giving me space to reflect on what I just said. I try to connect Ed's thoughts to something in my own life. Have there been situations where others' viewpoints about myself did not match up to my own, I wonder. Plenty of situations, I realize, including the management's thinking that I am the best person to drive this change initiative. I share this with Ed.

He considers this thoughtfully. 'Some of us overestimate our abilities leading to overconfidence and some of us tend to only focus on the negative aspects of ourselves, highlighting our weaknesses all the time, whilst disregarding our potential! This is generally the case in those with self-esteem issues. A balanced view on both positives and negatives is crucial in this situation'.

'Sometimes it is important to shift from only giving attention to those weaknesses we perceive, and take a moment to acknowledge our strengths. Acknowledging these strengths helps us to be grateful for who we are – a complete polar shift from low self-esteem', he comments.

We walk in silence for a minute; the sky is light blue now with white clouds reflecting the yellow rays of the sun.

'What a great privilege to be a part of this beauty!' Ed exclaims, admiring the sky as we continue to walk. 'Likewise, what a privilege it is to be grateful for who you are and what you have, both good and bad'.

We turn back at the hotel. The sea is rough here and the boulders make this stretch more picturesque than ever. Ed stops to greet a friend on the beach who is jogging and continues thereafter, 'Eventually, we all want to grow to be the best we can be. Awareness is critical for growth, which is why it is crucial in succeeding in any arena'.

I remain quiet as he continues. My thoughts are in constant motion this morning, I realize. But I feel incredibly present in the moment, like when I watch my kids play or smile in their sleep.

'Thank you so much for your time Ed. I'd like to walk with you more often if it's ok.', I say.

'Yes, let's meet next Saturday. Now you give it a good thought. Life's too short to go with the wave and whatever that uncertainty you are facing at work, might be a good thing. See what you can learn from it', Ed adds.

I smile in agreement and start to jog back home. For some reason, I feel more confident about facing the day.

....

Back at work

I design a survey to be distributed to the factory, managers, and the levels below. I cross-check this with my boss and roll it out.

At the same time, I entrust the job of collecting the data to a small team under me headed by my friend Naren. I personally carry out the focus group discussions amongst the machine operators.

Furthermore, we gather information from the recruitment team, induction team and training units, and all the documentation from exit interviews.

I am the first to report to work almost every day and the last to leave, weekends included.

It's been a hard day's night!

....

EAR FOR THY WORDS

It's a beautiful day and the stars are still visible in the weakening darkness of the morning. I have been a star-gazer; since my childhood, I have been fascinated by the mysteries beyond the skies.

From Aristotle, Copernicus, and Galileo to Hubble, Tombaugh and Gamow, I have a collection of books that I guard like gold. Stargazing is my hobby; it helps me to relax, fills me with awe, and reminds me how small my problems are.

So yes, before I bought myself a smart-phone, after a stressful day at work, my wife would find me in the balcony with my telescope. Having a complete beach view and living at the end of the lane has its perks. I am ashamed to say that setting up the telescope has become harder lately, now that I have an easier way to relax – social media. What a cheap trade off!

Star-gazing was my father's favorite pastime. As a young boy, I would sit on his lap and he would help me see bits of the constellations and tell me captivating tales about outer space. Those moments, watching the sky in the quietness of the night, built the strongest bonds between my father and myself. When I was fourteen years old, he had a sudden heart attack and passed away at 41 years of age. But I worked at it on my own. I found comfort by continuing to find wonder in the stars. It somehow helped me to stay connected to my father. To my horror and people's surprise, I never cried at his funeral.

As I stand watching the ocean, I hear the ruffling of the undergrowth behind me as someone walks towards me.

'Good morning Roy!' a friendly voice calls out from behind. Turning around, I see Ed. 'It looks like you've been waiting for me.'

'Good morning Ed! Yes, I was up from around three this morning. Sometimes, I just can't sleep at a stretch', I say.

'Ah ha! You are stressed!', he explains, to which I don't reply.

We start our brisk walk as the sea breeze blows over our way and swirls around us.

'Quite windy today', he comments. 'How was your week?'

'Last week was okay', I smile. 'I just tried to see things as they are without getting caught up in the drama. This walk with you helps. Thank you!'

'I'm glad you've been reflecting, Roy. How do you feel after all this thinking?', Ed asks.

After a few seconds, I reply, 'I feel more grounded and still inside now. At the beginning, I realized I lacked a sense of being anchored, but the more I reflected on who I was and what I wanted, the realizations themselves kept me focused; this has really helped me with the change at work'.

'I am glad Roy. Last week, we mainly spoke about being aware as a person which brings a sense of presence within you. Today, I want to talk about being present with another person', Ed says. 'Tell me, when you interact or talk with someone, how conscious are you of the other person?'

'I am conscious', I say. 'I think I am a good listener', I add.

'That's good!', Ed says encouragingly. 'I had a lot of work to do in that area. I often find myself jumping to conclusions and being so preoccupied with my own interpretation of the person or the situation, that I am unable to fully attend to what the other is saying', he confesses.

'I've never thought of communication in that way. It's always been something we just do, and should ideally do well', I tell Ed.

'Communication enables you to build a relationship with another individual. In good communication, you wholly understand yourself, your biases, and then go onto completely understand the person involved', Ed says. 'Good communication builds on our own awareness of where we could go wrong. It allows us to better understand another person when we are aware of our own beliefs, perceptions, attitudes, preconceptions and misconceptions about the other person or the situation', he adds.

Ed continues, 'Just yesterday at the new mall, I was accompanying my wife who wanted to skim through their latest collection of children's books. A flustered young mother who was fashionably dressed with several piercings and loud makeup, was looking for her child and came up to us to inquire. We had seen her a few minutes before in the shoe section totally engrossed with the shoes that she was trying on, one after the other. We had to excuse ourselves several times to walk past the pile of shoes and her bags that were laid on the floor', Ed narrates.

'What a careless mother!' I think with gratitude of my wife, who is so caring and responsible in how she looks after the children. My reverie is cut short as Ed continues.

'According to this lady, the child was only three years old. While she frantically related where she saw the kid last, and what the kid was wearing, I could not help but notice how I had already concocted a negative judgment about this lady as a careless mother', Ed says.

As I nod vigorously in agreement, I suddenly realize the shift in the story.

Ed continues, 'On the other hand, my wife's thoughts had immediately transitioned to problem solving mode, as she had come up with ways in which to find the child. At this moment, we both realized that we had missed out an important feature of the child, which was whether it was a boy or a girl she had lost. The way the mother described the child, we both concluded in our heads that this child was a boy but this was not the case. When the child was finally found hiding between long hanging dresses, we were both startled and my wife gasped. "I thought the child was a boy"'.

'I realized then how both my wife and I, in our own ways, had failed at really listening to and questioning the lady to help her find her child. I tell you Roy, the older you get, sometimes the more you think you know and the less you listen to others. I probably was not a good listener to begin with. Still a long way to go', Ed nods reflectively.

'Something comes to my mind Ed. A nursery rhyme that plays on a CD while my little girl who is four has her meals; it may sound childish but I am going to say it anyway. It goes like,

"The wise old owl lived in an oak,

The more he saw, the less he spoke,

The less he spoke the more he heard,

Why can't we all be like that wise old bird"', I finish, slightly awkwardly.

Ed smiles widely with delight, 'What a wonderful rhyme! That sums it all'.

I sometimes loathe these rhymes and ask my wife to stop the music as they keep repeating in my head even after leaving the house for work, while driving or even when I go to sleep. But today, I appreciate that I remember the lyrics.

We walk in silence for sometime before Ed starts a conversation again.

'Communication is very important for growth. Babies learn about the world by communicating with those around them. Just watch your infant play with a toy: how curious he is when he explores the object', Ed says.

'As you grow older, how you communicate and build relationships becomes the hallmark of what you are known for. So never underestimate the importance of the simple stuff!', Ed adds wisely.

'Last time, we spoke about the eye as the organ that represents awareness. What organ do you think best represents communication as we have just understood it?', Ed adds with a smile.

My mind immediately jumps to say 'mouth', but I stop myself. Wanting to give only the correct answer, I ponder on what Ed said. Communication is a means of truly understanding another person, was how Ed defined it.

'Ears', I reply confidently.

'Good! You can read my mind', Ed laughs. 'I think the ear is the most fitting organ to understand communication, as ideal communication should be more listening and less talking. The auditory system takes in information even during gestation, in the last 10-12 weeks of fetal development. That's how important communication is! Within the womb, we are exposed to sounds from the outside world, which is a form of connecting with others and gaining reassurance. There have been numerous reported cases of premature babies who, while fighting for life, had been exposed to familiar sounds such as the singing of their mother, and these have sparked significant recovery!'

The beach is filling up with more walkers now; these are all familiar faces, the morning walker community. We smile, nod, and greet others as we walk on towards the hotel.

Ed continues, 'The first thing I want you to draw your attention to is how it is structured. There is the inner ear, the middle ear, and the outer ear. The outer ear collects the sound waves, transfers it to the middle ear, and then they are transferred to the ear drum where they become nerve impulses that travel to the brain'.

By this point in our conversation, we have reached the end of the beach strip towards Colombo. A pier juts out into the ocean, and a group of boys is fishing; their youthful chitchat filling the air. I am awestruck as I see the sky, which is now a few shades of blue. Here, we pause for a moment, before Ed starts again.

'Do you mind sitting down for a while?', Ed asks.

Surprised, I say, 'Not at all'.

We sit down on the sand. Some throw curious glances our way, but avert their gaze as soon as they meet our eyes. Ed looks around, and then gestures behind us.

'Look at that couple', he says. 'What do you see?'

I watch for a few seconds and turn back. 'That woman is talking to that man, but he seems to be disconnected. He's looking elsewhere. She looks really unhappy. Must be a marital squabble', I say, recognizing the signs.

'Describe what you see. Tell me about the man', Ed invites me to speak further.

I look again for a few seconds and then respond, 'Well, he's not looking at her. Earlier he was staring at the restaurants, and now he is looking down. His arms are crossed. He keeps shifting his position'.

'Much better!', Ed approves. He starts looking around again, and then fixes his eyes on another pair on the beach. This pair is one of my acquaintances: a mother and a daughter.

'I know those two', I tell Ed. 'Really nice people! That entire family walks on the beach sometimes.'

'Now Roy, observe them and tell me what you see', says Ed ignoring my comments.

It is pleasant to watch. The mother speaks with her entire body. She moves her hands, and talks with energy. The little girl is listening with her entire body as well. She is leaning forward, watching her mother with enthusiasm. She reacts to something her mother says with liveliness, and seems so absorbed. I share this with Ed.

'Do you see the difference between this little girl and that man, Roy?', Ed asks. 'Look at the girl's posture. Her entire self is open in a way that you know she is listening. Structurally she is like the ear. It makes it easier for her to receive information. In contrast, the man is the opposite. He is what the ear would be if it was turned inward, and constantly moving. His posture is not conducive to receiving information'.

How true this is! It reminds me of what my wife says in the heat of some argument or other. When I avert my gaze, or fidget around (given the guilt/discomfort of the situation), she gets so frustrated that she asks me to listen properly!

Ed continues, 'That's the first thing we need to know during communication. To make ourselves truly present in the moment, and give our utmost concentration and attention to the speaker. The way we position our body, how we ask questions, our facial expressions, our body language, affect how we listen'.

'Yeah that makes sense', I add with eagerness. 'After all, not everyone communicates verbally. For those with speech/hearing impairments, visual cues are all they go by! Same story when we have to communicate with a foreigner'.

Ed laughs at my keenness, 'Once again, correct, Roy'.

'In my internship as a young doctor, and if I'm not mistaken, it was the surgical rotation in a rural hospital in the North. I didn't know any Tamil, and the community there spoke very little Sinhalese. Most of us, non-Tamil speakers had to rely on a nurse to interpret and translate to us which was not ideal', he relates.

'I remember feeling the distinct difference between attempting to diagnose a patient after speaking to them in Sinhalese versus in Tamil. When you speak to someone directly, you get the full picture; you can see how the pain is affecting them, you understand the emotions, you sense their essence, and you get the full understanding of what they are going through. This is not the case when someone gives you a rough interpretation of a patient's situation', Ed seems serious.

'That brings me to the crux of all this Roy. Building presence with a person, appreciating their situation, listening to them actively, understanding them completely, withholding your judgment, all this can be done very mechanically', Ed says.

'Really?', I ask, eager to hear more.

'Of course, without empathy, communication is mechanical. Numerous hotlines for customer service, you know what I mean; they are so very perfect and sometimes it feels so robotic'.

I can relate to that, yes.

He continues, 'Empathy comes from within us, and enables us to communicate with another person, truly and genuinely. Empathy means putting yourself in another person's shoes. It means living and breathing that person's situation as your own. I think, if we are able to tap into this quality, everything we spoke about this morning will come with no effort Roy'.

He gestures at the sand again, and we sit down cross legged and watch the sky: now a kaleidoscope of fading blue and ocher. Ed speaks again, 'Empathy allows us to communicate genuinely, and communicating genuinely enables us to empathize'.

We sit in silence for a few moments longer.

'Thank you Ed, for sharing that with me', I say, truly appreciating his time. 'I think I have my challenge for the week planned out now', I add smiling to myself.

'It is my pleasure. I believe that because it is coming from a genuine place of wanting to grow to be your best self, you would find this a fairly easy task. I look forward to hearing your stories from work next Saturday!'

'I hope all will go according to plan', I say in response.

'All the best Roy. It's now time for my walk alone'.

Ed gets up and starts walking back to where we started. I sit there and ponder for a while. Oh! How I wish I had the luxury of taking a break from work to just focus on all these precious lessons!

....

Back at work

We analyze the information and data from the surveys. When I show the results to my boss, he asks me to pay special attention to what the people have said about the management and asks me to do a needs-analysis based on it. He asks me to collect all the points necessary to talk to the target supervisor and line manager groups.

It is becoming overwhelmingly difficult and I could see the resistance more and more from HR.

In an unexpected conversation, my boss reveals to me that he has to leave for the US due to a family emergency, that he is contactable over the phone and for me to continue the work. He says he will be back in two weeks.

I request him to get some other senior manager, the GM or HR on board, but he says that it is not a good idea reiterating that this is how the owners want it and that it has to be done through this new unit of Change Management.

I urge him to make a formal announcement via an email to the entire factory to notify everyone about my new role (as they usually do). He says that he will do it before he leaves.

....

HAND FOR THY GRASP

Isn't it funny how certain people make their mark on our lives in a matter of a few meetings? It is only my third formal meeting with Ed, but I am feeling a connection to the man which is quite surreal, considering the short time I have known him.

In the past two instances, I had been there earlier than Ed. Today, he has beaten me to it.

We start walking towards the hotel, southwards.

As we walk, Ed starts to talk, picking up from last week. 'Let's build on something we spoke about last week; from communication to connection. Everything and everyone is connected, some directly and some indirectly. Look at the sky, the sea, the earth, and the two of us. In this moment and in this place, this colossal connection is real. If there is a natural connection, we unite with persons, places and things to remain grounded and present', Ed continues.

'The point about cohesiveness is very crucial here. Think of your hand for example; how many bones do you think it consists of?', he asks.

'I'm clueless!', I say.

Ed responds, 'Twenty-seven bones in the skeleton of the hand. There are many individual parts- each finger, the palm, the knuckles, the wrist. They are all connected to each other given the many connecting fibers. But if I ask you to pick up that branch on the beach,' Ed says pointing towards a branch from a nearby tree. 'You would need each part of the hand to work together cohesively and as one unit'.

We walk on, and I think of the focus group discussions I need to conduct for the change initiative.

Ed continues, 'In human relationships, trust is absolutely essential. Trust, trust, trust, we cannot emphasize it enough'.

We trail along for a while. I ponder over the word trust. It is common knowledge that trust is difficult to build and easy to break. Personally, I take some time before I can trust someone. It is only after getting to know a person well that I am able to trust them. Thereafter, I trust them completely.

I remember my wife's infectious laughter in the first couple of months of our acquaintance, when she could not get me to open up. She would constantly liken me to secretive characters in her favorite novels. She would tease me for having such strongly guarded walls. When I finally caved in, she was so surprised to see how much I trusted and opened up. 'It's like the flood gates have opened', were her exact words.

'Ed…', I start. 'I have a question along the lines of what we were discussing'.

'Tell me Roy', Ed encourages.

'Well I was thinking, it's quite difficult to connect with groups of people, or even individuals, who are different to you. Yet you were able to fit in and do wonders in a business setting even though you had been immersed in the medical background for so many years. That's quite impressive! How did you manage that?', I ask.

'That is very kind of you Roy to say so. Well, first thing is I didn't pretend to be anyone I wasn't. I didn't have much knowledge on business theory. I never pretended to know what I didn't. Your authenticity, who you are genuinely, is your greatest tool to connect with any group Roy!'

I nod quietly. 'But you would have been so different from them, right? And like you said, there was a knowledge gap as well. So, how did you not only fit in with them, but also do so well?', I ask.

'Aha! That is my trade secret Roy!', Ed grins charmingly. 'I worked with what I knew. I had very little knowledge of how organizations worked. When I worked with these business guys, I taught them lessons from the best example of an organization there is!'

'Which is?', I ask, piqued with curiosity.

'The human body, of course!', Ed responds happily. 'As a doctor, my greatest strength was a good understanding of how the human body works, and how it responds to situations of adversity. I used lessons from the body, and my position as a doctor, to help these business guys make sense of the issues in the organization'.

I am speechless.

'The human body as a business model?' I utter in astonishment.

Ed continues, 'When we try to connect with a group Roy, whether it's a small group or a large audience, our biggest tool is our true self. So you need to keep it real and most of the time, simple. You needn't try to be anybody else. When you are genuine, and drawing from yourself, it shows, and that helps groups connect with you. On the contrary, if you are trying to be someone else, a know-all, the inconsistencies show. This makes it difficult for a group to trust you'.

He is thoughtful for a few moments, and then adds, 'What also helps is to find some common ground between you and others. When you find this common ground, it provides a foundation for the relationship to be built on'.

I nod quietly in response.

'Let me give you an example. My wife and I love stand-up comedy and we are both marveled by how some people have this uncanny ability to make people laugh. It's harder to make people laugh than to make them cry', he says.

'So when we were newly married and living in the UK with no massive commitments as such, we used to go to the local pub that hosted some of the wittiest comedians in town. One day in winter, there was a contest for the young and upcoming stand-up comedians and the pub was packed with people. One after the other, the contestants performed; some funny, some not-so-funny. But it was a wonderful night. And before they declared the winners, the hosts announced that there was one more contestant who had just arrived and asked the crowd whether they should give him the opportunity, even though he was almost an hour late. Of course, we agreed', Ed reminisces, smiling.

'But there was something about this young man; he seemed quite ordinary in his over-sized jacket, compared to the ones who had already performed. When given the microphone, he didn't seem to be confident and was looking down. With every passing second, people were not expecting much and then suddenly while looking down he mentioned "It's cold. I'm shivering inside out of stage fright"', Ed narrates.

'People laughed and then he finally looked up and smiled warmly at everyone and said "I completed three years at Cambridge but never graduated because I had cold feet at my viva"', Ed laughs in memory.

'Then, this seemingly nervous young man started to make fun of his own fears and insecurities, and for most of us, in some way or the other, we saw ourselves in the small snippets of the stories he related so cleverly in the most humorous way one could ever imagine. We connected because he was real, because he gave us something to trust, such as a piece of his own life story. We all ended up laughing almost at ourselves, at our prides, our own over-confidence, our own education, credentials and titles. In that moment in the pub, we all became human beings because of a young man who entertained us on our own vulnerabilities', Ed finishes.

'That's a cool story, but who would want to study for three years in Cambridge and then quit...', I wonder aloud.

'Well, life oh life! Be it Cambridge or a local college, we make choices that we think are right for us given the circumstances', Ed says, alerting me to recognize my judgmental tone.

We walk on quietly for a while. I watch the other walkers on the beach. There are some small groups that generally jog together. I suppose they too come together based on some shared factor. Maybe they live close by, play a sport together, went to school together, or work together. Connections are made due to shared values, shared cultures and beliefs, shared ambitions, goals, and similarities. Those fishermen with the nets; their profession binds them together.

Ed's voice breaks the silence, 'I once had to testify in courts to prove myself innocent. I realized that the only thing I could do was to be honest and to ensure everyone in the courtroom could see how sorry I was. Even though there was much anger at the beginning, there was a shift later on, when people started to empathize with me'.

I notice the slight deflation in his usual self. I want to know more, but realize it is not the time to get down to the nitty gritty of the issue.

The sea is calm today, and the sound of the waves is almost therapeutic.

'The willingness to be vulnerable is a crucial aspect of making connections in a group. When people realize you are merely human with a set of weaknesses just like theirs, they trust you because you don't act perfect. However, they can always abuse this knowledge of your weaknesses; that's the risk you take. In my case, I directly told everyone present at the courts what I did not know, and how imperfect I was as a human being. You see the thing is, it has to come from a place of confidence. When you know who you are, and that your identity is tied to something much bigger than your mere appearance, skills and knowledge, title, or your own experience, you are not afraid to admit that you don't know some things', Ed reflects.

A murder of crows, believe it or not, are ousting what appears to be a small eagle. The sound of these common creatures fills the air; a blanket of features chasing after a lone wanderer. Both Ed and I stop and watch the commotion before we start walking again.

'We need people; people and relationships protect us. As a team you could do so much more. As a team, fighting adversity becomes easier. People and connections protect us from loneliness, depression and many other diseases. It can create a ripple effect in the community. In the absence of this, societies and businesses become painfully self-focused, suspicious, and slow in effectiveness and productivity, as you work in an environment where the priority becomes to first protect yourself. This leads to unsafe and insecure cultures', concludes Ed.

I think to myself; the Town Hall meeting is coming up this week and I realize the success of it would vastly depend on how I will make a connection with the audience as a facilitator. Hard times are ahead; but the outcome is ultimately based on how I would make them feel.

Ed stops to face the ocean, and looks towards the horizon. I mirror his pose.

'Great then! I think that should be it for today! Reflection time for Ed now. I shall see you next week Roy!' Ed says happily.

'Okay Ed. See you next Saturday!'

Ed waves at me, and starts pacing away. I start walking towards the opening from which I entered the beach this morning. I wonder what this week would bring my way.

··

Back at work

No formal announcement has been made yet about my role but my boss has sent an email to all the participating managers asking them to be present at the meeting where I would be speaking.

At work I find it increasingly difficult to answer everyone's questions, and I find myself surrounded by a vibe of suspicion and doubt; fake smiles and annoyed looks from colleagues who joined the company as management trainees. I have several calls unanswered on my phone and I detest looking at the screen as it rings. Whenever someone is open to discussion, I explain the scope of the initiative and reassure them that everyone will get an opportunity and the resources to change. That ultimately, it will be a win-win, I hope.

'Yeah right!' is some people's reaction to me. I fail to think straight, as I am engulfed in a grape vine that is spreading at uncontrollable speed. I am bombarded by calls from the other factories, as everyone, including those who hold higher positions, are curious to know how people are responding to my project. I feel as if I am in the midst of a horrific controversy, unprecedented and out of control.

On Friday at the Town Hall meeting, I find myself staring at the chairs an hour before the meeting is due to start. I am struck by the realization, that in an hour or so, all these chairs would be filled with people; people with their own dreams, own families, with children who would be going to school today believing that tomorrow will be no different to any other day, and that their safety and security are guaranteed thanks to their parents' jobs.

How am I to actually convey this message? How will I tell these people that their jobs may be at risk if they don't change? A mix of emotions and feelings rush through me. I feel totally unqualified to be there. Deep down, this is not something I want to do. I feel like a messenger boy, the harbinger of distress. I think of some of the instances when my friends told me, 'Just say no; just say you can't do it! You can get another job'. In hindsight, I wonder if I should have heeded their advice.

My boss is supposed to appear on a conference call to convey the critical aspects of the initiative and I wait impatiently for him to connect online. I send him a few text messages and he suddenly calls on my mobile.

'Roy, you've got to go ahead and let them know. I have sent you a recording of the message I want to convey. My daughter is in hospital and I need to be there in 30 minutes. Hey, you are my man! Get this thing over and done with and get to the real work', he hangs up.

I am shocked at his behaviour; this is downright unacceptable. I try to focus on what needs to be done.

I feel my heart pounding in my chest as I feel weighed down by the immense responsibility I have to bear for these people. I pace up and down, grab a bottle of water, and sip it slowly. I pray under my breath for courage. I pray this initiative would be for the best for everyone; that this would be something everyone would embrace. I pray that everyone sees that this has the potential to change their lives in a good way.

Not wanting to be there alone, I call the GM of the plant. He does not answer and his secretary says that he is on leave the whole week. I call the Head of HR and he tells me that he is at the head office and that I should probably do what my boss has asked me to do.

I open the clip sent by my boss only to find out that it is a basic message. It ends with him palming off the responsibility to me to explain the process. I am angered by this message and I call one of my former bosses who is now working in another plant. He tells me what the Head of HR has told me, that I should do what my boss has asked me to do. In confidence he adds that I should not mess with his directives as he is highly connected. 'Corporate slaves we are', I tell him infuriated. He laughs and says, 'Yes we are, Roy. We have no choice sometimes'.

I think of how to word my first sentences. How ironic —how could I justify that losing their jobs might be a good thing?

I watch with trepidation as the chairs fill up. As people walk in to the hall and take their seats, I sense heavy clouds over the entire premises. I feel as if I know what each one is thinking – what they are thinking of me. 'Look at this young, unqualified brat! The audacity to tell us what our fate will be!'

Some of these people used to be my supervising managers when I was a Management Trainee. How am I to deliver this message to them?

When I look at the audience, I see a mixture of faces; some seem nervous, others wearing a façade. They plaster a smile of pretense of being okay, despite the fact that they are not. I take a deep breath, and again, to steady myself for what is to follow.

Despite my good intentions, my good will, and my sense of responsibility, things go wrong. As I start the presentation, I realize that I am overwhelmed with a sense of nervousness; I am so nervous that I dive in without making a connection.

I greet them straight away, briefly acknowledge that they know why they are gathered here, and play the clip my boss has sent. Thereafter, I promptly proceed to speak to them about the findings from the research study. I focus on the Power Point slides, with numbers and comments.

As I reach the third slide, a wave of realization slams on to me. As it sinks into me what I had done, or failed to do, I feel too scared to look into the faces of the managers.

Knowing I need to face the truth, I fearfully turn my gaze at the audience to gauge their reactions. I clearly see the frowns on some faces, in others', I see expressions suggesting the numbness, the shock, and disgust.

It has only been ten minutes since I started, and already people are leaving the hall one by one.

'This is some kind of a joke', I hear one say.

'Where is your boss, why can't he be here?', another shouts as someone pulls him to his seat alerting him that the walls have ears and that even though he is not present, given his connection to the founders, things could go from bad to worse.

Fifteen minutes into the meeting, more than half the people are gone.

Once again, I am struck by the gravity of the mistake I have made, but it's too late to turn back the clock.

I guiltily think of everything Ed has told me to date. What do I have to show for the lessons he shared? Everything he told me about communicating? Body language? About building trust? About assuring people of their worth? About opening up to be vulnerable first?

The enormity of my ignorance hits me over and over again. I'm disgusted with myself.

I'm tired; this whole experience feels like a working man's PhD.

HEART FOR THY PULSE

I just can't fall asleep. The baby has been crying the whole night, so my wife has been awake. I would have been able to use my time better if I was in the office room. Fear, angst, guilt; I did not want to go through with this. I'm not cut out to be courageous; I want to quit. I'm just a normal guy – the type of guy who would go to work, come home, maybe play with my kids when I feel up to it, read, or go to the balcony and gaze at the stars. The last is my favorite – studying the planetary world. That's who I am. Why would I run away from this identity?

Maybe it's a bubble; but what if I like my bubble?

I go downstairs and watch the news on all the news channels, till finally it is time for my walk.

As I approach the railway tracks this morning, I feel unsure as to why I was taking this walk with Ed in the first place. What could Ed give me? Maybe it's better for me to live life as it is, the way I can, the way I know how. Do I really need someone else telling me what life is, what I should be, how I should be, and why I should be a particular way? Am I willing to put this into practice?

I see Ed approaching at the end of the road, and I cannot help but greet him with negativity in my voice.

'Hi Ed, good morning! I don't know about you, but I am feeling too tired today'.

Ed looks at me intently and replies 'Good morning! You don't have to take this walk if you are not up to it. You can go home and rest'.

But for some reason, as I hear his words, I realize he has come on a Saturday just to continue our conversation.

So I change my mind and tell him in return, 'It's okay Ed. Maybe this walk would do me good. Maybe I need to take some time to catch my breath and put things straight...'

I glance at Ed, and from his expression, I reckon Ed has instinctively realized that something was wrong.

He is quiet. As we trundle along, he adds in a gentle voice, 'You know Roy, you don't really have to listen to my stories. I am not sure what you will gain out of this. You don't have to take this walk'.

As he speaks, I notice that his voice is so fatherly, so calm. At this moment, I decide that this is probably what I want and what I need right now.

And so we continue the walk, and I tell him, 'Look Ed, I am going to be completely honest with you. Sometimes I wonder why I have to change. I wonder whether things would be better if I could just, you know, not worry too much about what's happening at work. If I could say no, and just hand in my resignation. I could apply for another job. I have a decent amount of savings. It's not going to be that bad. I really don't know why I have to go through this'.

After a brief silence, Ed starts to speak in reply.

He answers, 'What if everything happens for a reason; that our lives are unique, that we can't actually compare ourselves with others? And that every problem we face is common, yet so personal in nature? What if in this journey, you have a choice – to quit, or to walk? What if you can decide whether you want to give up now, and just get a job that will keep you happy, devoid of drama for a while, until it becomes tough to deal with and you quit again. And then you just settle down with a job that makes you complacent, say to become a cog in the wheel'.

He continues, 'But what if you could also look at this in terms of the bigger picture? Change is inevitable and as we speak now, we change even at a cellular level; the scenery before us changes as people come and people go; even those humongous rocks change with every splashing wave'.

'Ask yourself, what will you do now, now that the resources are limited and you need to step up to a new level? Not just in your doing, but also in your thinking? What if it is drive that you need from within when things are not going well?'

His words challenge my thinking and I struggle to wrap my thoughts around what he just said. We walk in silence.

Ed continues, 'This drive is a form of energy within us. It could be positive or negative. From a negative perspective it could arise from guilt, a wish to avoid punishment, fear, or to prove a point or keep up with the Joneses. On the other hand, this drive can be a life force. It could be the motivation that is needed for you to wake up in the morning and do something above and beyond your circumstances', he adds seriously.

'You see Roy, I'm no guru, but I probably have lived long enough to relate to this desire you have to quit, because you're tired, weary, and cannot take it anymore. But son, if you can't go any further, just stay where you are now for a while, and then see what could be done. Don't be quick to quit. You don't want to regret over this decision one day', he finishes, kindly.

Did he just call me 'son'? A pleasant surprise. I remain silent, absorbing fervently everything Ed says.

'You see, "drive" is like this heart that pumps blood to the rest of the body. The heart pumps blood that provides the body with oxygen, and it helps remove wastes. See, this headquarters of the circulatory system is a miracle machine; it only stops when we die', he laughs.

'You know what I love about this heart? It is disciplined. In a healthy heart, blood flows one way due to heart valves, which prevent backflow. The motivation and drive of a person should be disciplined. It should be in constant flow; it should move to enrich and nourish the purpose and remove the waste and toxins that can obstruct the circulation', Ed adds.

Strangely, I am fascinated.

Ed looks at me carefully, and says encouragingly, 'Roy, maybe you are discouraged right now. But if you really look at it, you don't have much of a choice, as you have already chosen to be greater than your current circumstances. At work, this is why you asked for more challenge from your boss at your feedback session. Today, that is why you chose to walk with me despite the tiredness'.

His voice turns somber, and I see a flicker of the sadness I saw the last time, when Ed mentioned the court case. He says, 'You see, in my life drive has both killed and redeemed me; *killed me* because I was too ambitious, too determined, that I just couldn't understand why I had to be that striving. Maybe it was to prove something to myself. I never wanted to stop. If I stopped, my brain would still work in the night; I would sleep with questions; I would feel my brain whirring away, solving problems. It wouldn't rest. As a doctor, my desire was to increase my impact; not just in my own practice and as a specialist, but I wanted to reach out to many people and increase my influence. Of course, the understanding of true impact and influence came later. But in the earlier years, my focus was on getting promoted, gaining titles, and proving myself worthy'.

I try to imagine a younger Ed, thirsty for success, but my attempts are cut short as Ed continues his story.

'The best thing is, my "drive" up to date has not stopped – it's working like my heart that hasn't stopped yet. It's beating – sometimes slowly, sometimes fast. It's like I've come to the end of a finish line in a marathon; you are almost there, yet you are still a few lengths away', he says.

He pauses for a moment, catching his breath and continues, 'This drive helped me to understand different people from different walks of life. I was able to, in the way I knew how, to bring about healing using the knowledge and medical advancements that were available to us. It was this drive that kept me awake and alert and helped me to do delivery after delivery long hours into the night, sometimes not taking time to even have my lunch or a snack. I still remember sometimes while in surgery, I would feel the hunger – only to realize that this pang was hardly bothering me at all, because what was in front of me, that mission to deliver a child to the world, was so much bigger and more powerful than any discomfort I was facing'.

I suddenly think of my wife, and wonder how she would feel if my ambition took over my health. As it is, she is distressed that I don't take enough care of myself. I decide to veer the topic off course slightly.

'Tell me about your wife Ed, how did you meet her and how did she respond to all this?' I ask curiously.

Ed grins, 'It all began in the UK. I got married late because I just did not have time to meet people. I met her at a medical conference. She was a physiotherapist, but I realized she was not enjoying her work much'.

'She was a great match for me; quiet and patient. But she was too sensitive and somewhat stubborn. I used to think that she was a complicated person to begin with, and would to tell her all the time that men don't understand women - that it could be true that men are from Mars and women are from Venus', he laughs.

'You see, I had this aspiration to have our own family clinic. It was a dream I could entrust to no one – so I asked her to join me. She had her own clinic at the time, smart one that she is. She had been based in the UK much longer than I. We took a mortgage and bought the building next to it to expand. We created a space for medical doctors to come and consult', Ed says, thoughtfully.

'It was the busiest of times', he comments. 'I was busy with all the hospital visits, and would clock in almost 14 hours of work a day, and then would go to the clinic to check on everything. I would not get much time to spend with my son who was only a few months at the time. For us it was the wrong time to start our own business as there was too much change. In hindsight, I would have done things differently. I would have taken time to enjoy my son's childhood, and he is our only son you see', Ed adds with a sense of regret.

'We were living on rent at that time, as all our savings were invested on securing the building for the clinic. My wife was the only one I trusted when it came to business; so I asked her to manage both her clinic and our joint clinic. She was reluctant at the beginning as she was still on maternity leave, but I think she didn't have much of a choice as I can be very persistent about what I want', Ed reflects.

I can't help but sense the sadness in his voice.

Ed continues, 'You see Roy, I was and still am a perfectionist, and our styles of working are so different. She would take it easy and that's how I saw it then, and she would never say "no" to people. Even though I considered her to be sharp and intelligent, I felt more professional firmness was required from her when managing people; and I kept telling her this', Ed says thoughtfully.

He pauses, and stares at the horizon. He continues, 'I am sure I came across as nagging and bossy, as if I thought I knew better, and as if I were the one dictating the terms. The worst thing was, in retrospect, I never even listened to the issues she had to manage, I mean "people" issues. For me it's a given; "people" issues are always there, but one must know to choose their battles. For me, it was that simple because I wasn't the one managing it. Even if I were to do it, it would be very cut and dry, whereas she would be too nice, so I thought. And being too nice had never made anyone successful'.

Ed draws his gaze away from the waves of the ocean to look at me. 'This was taking a toll on our marriage', he comments and continues.

'We should have taken the time to be just us. But instead, over time, we became more and more distant. Our conversations were always about work, consultants, equipment, clients – something she would always point out. I would never take much heed. Our child, at the time, was around one and a half years old - quite young. From three weeks of age, he was taken to the clinic, to a small nursery I got my wife to create at the back of the facility so that she could still keep an eye on the operations. She hated it and said that all I cared about was this clinic of ours. And after six months, the baby would go to the créche four days a week for a few hours and my wife would take a day off to be with him once a week'.

He continues, 'What frustrated me most about my wife was that I felt she was overpromising what she couldn't deliver. I have quite high standards; at the very least, I expect promises to be delivered on time, and she was failing to do this. I would always say, "You have the mind of an artist. You're all muddled up in your thoughts, you say one thing, but you do something else". Maybe I was right – and my wife *was* all that, but I should have excused her, knowing that she had several roles to play; a mother (and she never compromised on that), a wife to an authoritative perfectionist, physiotherapist, and a manager of the clinic', Ed says.

He gestures to the beach, and we sit down on the sand, facing the endless ocean.

'She was a good physiotherapist, and had a long list of people waiting to get an appointment with her. She was a good artist; she always wanted to write children's books, and had many manuscripts, which she never had the courage to publish. I pushed her and pushed her, and she would always reply "soon, not yet"', Ed reflects. 'You see what's sad about this was, I never took the time to read a single story she had written. It never crossed my mind. I mean, what busy doctor would read children's books, right?'

I smile weakly in response. The twinge of emotion in Ed's voice is unmistakable now.

'We would have huge arguments about how the clinic should be managed, and looking back, I think I was asking too much of her. At this time, we still didn't have a house of our own, which I think was important to her. During this time, we had to move houses once or twice due to distance and space and she hated it', Ed admits.

'After some time, all these issues built up to a level where she was talking to me less and less. She only spoke to me when it was needed. We communicated mainly through emails, because I insisted that everything should be documented in writing when it came to work. More and more, I found a reason not to spend time with my family; I found a reason to absorb myself in the work of the expansion of the clinic in another suburb as well. I want to say this now; it was not about money, it was about checking off the list of achievements and life goals I had set out to accomplish', Ed recollects.

After a few moments of silence, Ed starts again, his voice quieter than ever, barely audible above the crashing waves.

'After a while, she stopped speaking to me altogether'.

I feel the weight of Ed's story – his usually smiling eyes are serious and fixed on the ocean. We remain silent for a while, probably the longest silence to date.

Finally, Ed speaks. 'I tried to get her to talk; I kept telling her, "this is not good – this is damaging us, our family", and she wouldn't say anything in return'.

'I was so frustrated; I was convinced that she was being stubborn; she was someone who somehow made sure things went her way, or so I thought, but I was only describing myself there', Ed smiles sadly.

'You see, there was a lot of pain at the time for her I think. I was just not there for her, perhaps when she needed me the most. And I convinced myself that her struggles were too much to understand, that it would require time and energy that I simply could not afford to give. I brushed these nagging thoughts under the carpet again and again, until finally one night the consequences became clear', Ed says quietly.

Ed's voice is strained, but resolute. 'I walked into the house that night, and realized it was oddly still. It may have been close to mid-night. On the dining table, was a letter – addressed to me, neatly written by hand. She had left me'.

My mind struggles to wrap itself around these words. A wave crashes loudly on the shore.

Ed continues, 'The letter was too brief. It said, "You are a good man Ed, but I can't be who I'm not. I'm going home. I'm sorry"'.

'Just like that, she was gone. I felt numb', Ed continues somberly. 'I could not think of anything. For the first time in my life, I felt what it meant to not think. I should have called the hospital to cancel all my surgeries. But I didn't do that. On the one hand, I felt life had to go on, and that if I stayed home doing nothing, it would break me, ruin me. I thought, I would do what I am supposed to do', Ed narrates.

'Then I also felt, it was she who had left. If it was okay with her, well it should be okay with me. And so I went to work. I did that faithfully the next morning, and the morning after that', Ed smiles at me grimly.

The blowing is strong today.

'Yet there was so much anger within me, directed towards her; how could she do this to me? Leave *me*? How could she unilaterally decide to separate me from *my* child? This anger was all consuming and blowing out of proportion within me. The after-taste of failure that someone has almost betrayed you, abandoned you, and left you high and dry to find your own answers consumed me. What was I to think? But then there were times when I realized that I had withdrawn into a shell within me, and I was quieter than ever before', he reflects.

'As always Roy, your decisions come back to bite you in the back. For me, it was my decision to go back to work despite what had happened; my decision to push aside the events, not confront it or let it sink in', Ed says.

I look at him questioningly. He nods once.

'I was very secretive about everything. Nobody knew what had happened except my wife's secretary at the clinic. She was an old lady, and she told me, "Ed you've got to stop. Go and get her. This is enough. You're 42; don't ruin your life. You've worked so hard to build it. Make things right!" I refused to listen to her well-meant words. After all, I justified, who was she? Just a lonely secretary. A neighbor. Unmarried, too. What would she know about marriage? About ambition? About my bigger vision?', he recounts.

Ed remains in silence for nearly two minutes, deep in thought.

My heart beats fast in my chest, as if I am right now living in this story, experiencing it with the man next to me.

Unable to contain my curiosity, I ask 'So what happened Ed?'

Ed smiles somewhat sadly and continues, 'It was a Wednesday. It was three days after she had left. It may have been around seven thirty in the evening, and I went into the theatre for a C- Section'.

His voice drops, 'I had been in and out of the theater for almost 6 hours that day, and this lady was brought in, pregnant with twins, multiple complications and nearly six months into her pregnancy. But that day, something crazy happened. With good intentions I attempted something I should not have'.

'During the emergency caesarean, I realized the presence of a nine centimeter fibroid embedded in the upper wall of the uterus, away from the caesarean cut. Neither its position nor its size was obstructing the surgery and I could have easily ignored it, but I decided to remove the fibroid because the mother's condition was stable. However, I was breaching safety limitations and I was aware of it. Nevertheless, I took the risk. Well! I don't want to go into details, but my decision led to the mother bleeding to death'.

Silence and silence. Then he speaks again.

'One twin died immediately and the other twin succumbed after two weeks. But both the deaths were not related to the death of the mother. They had been under-developed, even for six months'.

More silence. I did not have the heart to ask him to continue, even though I desperately wished he would.

He begins to speak again, 'They stopped me from practicing immediately. In the inquiry within the hospital and the one the Medical Council carried out, they decided that I was not psychologically fit to practice because of the recent separation with my wife'.

Should I say something? I struggle with a lack of words to speak.

The sound of the waves are now amplified in my ears.

Ed speaks after a while.

'The patient's gynecologist was out of the country, as he had not expected a premature delivery. My patient was highly connected and was the daughter of a well-known lawyer in London. The nurse insisted that she mentioned this to me before surgery but up-to-date, I fail to recall that piece of information being mentioned to me prior to surgery. Not that it should have made any difference, but what transpired after that point had much to do with their standing in society'.

Ed's face is a mask of remorse and distress. My heart thuds in my chest, anxious. And then he speaks again.

'Just like that, the mother who was 27 years old, and her twins were gone. In the moments after the surgery, I remember demanding, "Why would you bring someone so high profile to me when there are more senior doctors in this hospital working in the same hour?" She was not a patient of mine and I had limited knowledge about her history of complications. The response I got was the worst thing that could have happened after such a terrible loss', Ed looks at me with a bitter smile.

'See Roy, what I was told in response were the very words I had dreamt of hearing as a junior doctor many years ago, working hard, building my career skill by skill. What I was told was "You are one of the very few surgeons in London who could have handled such multiple complications at the time"'.

'These were the words of my dream Roy, and after a blissful second when I realized what I had been told, my next realization led me to a complete disappointment in myself. What's the point in being the best when your carelessness had cost a human life and brought an end to your profession forever?', he says with emotion.

It looks like Ed's entire physique is screaming in distress. What happened to the man with the boundless joy?

'I had heard what I had been waiting to hear throughout my career, now, when my career was just about to end; a bitter lesson to this over-confident, heroic doctor', Ed adds.

'It was an ugly litigation but a simple one. My career, everything I had invested on during my entire life was gone. I lost my license to practice. I was sent for counseling for six months leading up to the final hearing', Ed says.

'I remember about two days after I got suspended, I couldn't take it anymore. I realized I wasn't as strong as I thought I was, so I tried to find my wife. I called her ancestral home here in Dehiwela, and tried to find her whereabouts, and finally found out she was living in an annex not very far from here', Ed says, gesturing to the vicinity.

'And then I called her, told her what happened, and you know what she told me? She said "Come home". You see Roy, I'm telling this to you because your drive, if not managed, if your ambition is not channeled in the right path towards priorities, sooner or later this river of an ambition would flood. It will destroy the dams that you've built, the communities that you have served and the people around you', Ed concludes with sadness.

'So did you come home immediately?', I ask. These are the first words I have spoken in what feels like the longest period of time.

He replies with a nod, 'Yes. I came home. Not immediately, as I had to wait for the case to be over. It took six months. During that time of waiting, I sold our clinics to the person who my wife had handed over her clients to; the lawsuit settlement cost almost all that money. And then I came home, because I had nothing else to do. And when I got home, I realized my son was talking now. And my wife looked so much younger; just six months and much had changed'.

His voice shifts, his posture straightens a bit, and when he speaks, some of the smile is back in his voice. 'Then another chapter in my life began; a journey of wholeheartedness. I had to change Roy. I had had enough of who I had been – that ambitious, ruthless man. I sold the only property my mother had left for me and built my wife a house, a home so to say. I took the time to know her better, and to listen to her when she spoke. The first few months, I read all her children's books, contacted a publisher in the UK, and got her books out there. I connected with my son better, played with him and brought him to this beach almost every day until I was offered a job'.

Ed stands up, and I follow. He brushes off the sand from his trousers and looks at me. 'You're probably horrified after hearing this story. I never thought of bringing this up, but, well, maybe that's what you needed to hear today'.

Finally, I comment on the unexpectedness of what Ed has shared.

'Ed, I don't know what to say', I admit.

Ed smiles back at me, the fatigue of sharing his story clear in his eyes. 'Don't worry, you said you were tired Roy. I'm going to continue this walk. Maybe you can go home and get some rest. Maybe that's the right thing to do for yourself'.

I nod, manage a smile and say, 'I truly appreciate what you shared, and all you have shared in the past few walks, the few times we have met. I will see you next Saturday Ed'.

Something shifts within me as a result of that meeting, and I don't know what it is. When I reach home, I go straight to my office room. I lock the door behind me to nap on the couch, and as I doze off, I think on how simple yet complicated life is.

As I wake up, I am unable to understand the nature of my feelings. My mind is cluttered, blocked, dysfunctional. I feel like a zombie.

Throughout the weekend, I am aloof. My wife repeatedly asks me if I'm okay. The kids laugh, cry, play, scream and do all the things they usually do. And I am left unable to process it.

That Monday before work, I walk on the beach alone. I recollect my thoughts, and become increasingly conscious that I have yet not figured out what to do about the dilemma at office. My boss had told me that I needed to figure something out soon.

I start running, finding it difficult to contain the pressure and anxiety I am feeling inside. I run as fast as I can, as if I'm racing against time.

Speed, more speed! My knees resisting the impact and the pain traveling all the way up the body.

The pain I feel in my body seems to momentarily compensate the ambiguity I feel inside. It is good, I tell myself. I feel alive as I feel the bone-breaking pain.

Just then, I knock against a fisherman running towards a boat with a can of fuel. I stop and turn around as I feel the thud on my right shoulder; it's almost as if it was done on purpose.

Then I realize something; something important.

I realize that in order to break this news to the managers one-to-one, that I need to be okay with one thing and one thing alone.

And that was, whether I was okay with losing my job; whether I was ready to take a hit if someone communicates that to me. Almost like an epiphany, it occurs to me.

....

Back at work

As I go to work, I feel a strong sense of readiness to speak to the 85 people, one by one, and I keep telling myself that I could be the 86th person going home. I take my list out.

I make a conscious decision, and put away the research; I don't need this for the meetings. I know the contents through and through anyway. I messed this up once; today, I just need to connect with them, speak to them, as if they were my friends, my brothers.

The meetings start, and I try to channel as much genuineness as I can into my encounters. I speak with them one by one, I sincerely apologize for the earlier meeting, and if I had come across in the wrong manner.

I emphasize that I am not here as a person waiting to get rid of them, but someone who is trying to do what is being expected of him.

In the middle of a conversation, I find myself subtlety challenging some managers to relook at their strengths and the sense of purpose as leaders. I encourage them to step up to the new changes when appropriate. But this is all done after establishing a sense of trust to have their best interest at heart.

Some meetings take long but I decide not to check the time. That day, I personally cover about one-tenth of the group that was present at the meeting.

I tell them to be open; I encourage them to speak out their feelings. I am amazed to find that people actually want to speak about how they feel. Some tear up; the ones who have given so much to the company thinking that in return they would be looked after, the ones who have no idea why this is imposed on them, the ones who are tired of complaining, and the ones who really want to go. I hear much negativity towards the management, sometimes about specific people and mostly about my very charismatic boss and his favourites. Some tell me that I am one of his favourites too and that is why I have been given this task.

However, what I notice most are the deeper concerns, the true emotions of fear; fear of loss of income, fear of not being able to provide for their families, their children; the fear of losing their identity as a breadwinner in the case of men, fear of losing face in society, the car they leased or the house they built on a loan that needed to be paid every month. The fear of not being good enough, not being respected anymore as it feels like they are being handpicked with an ultimatum.

I find some managers to be very sensitive to the feedback they hear. They tell me that their deliverables, are unrealistic at times and pressurizing their lines happens almost unconsciously.

In the absence of a possible solution that I could provide for their concerns, I start to ask questions to draw out the answers from them and over a few chats I realize I am getting better at it. More people leave energized and hopeful about change and how they can use this juncture in the career for their betterment.

I take it one day at a time, and by the end of two weeks, I have completed all eighty-five conversations. The outcome fills me with tremendous confidence, affirming that I have taken the right path and tackled the conversations the right way, because I too was ready for the risk of being made redundant.

At the end of these two weeks, my boss who is still away instructs me to call for another meeting, and all 85 people attend once more. This time, I know that whilst there is still some insecurity, they are confident about the information they now have. Most of the attendees have already thought of a plan B, and they have some awareness of their own weaknesses and areas of development.

This for me is as ideal an outcome as it could have been – too good to be true. During these chats, I feel a sense of trust developing that I honestly cannot attribute a reason to. All I can do is to be grateful that this is the case.

....

SPINE FOR THY FORM

A week after our last conversation, Ed and I meet again on the beach, doing our usual walk. This time, I see him differently. It is as if he has aged. Funny, it is not that he has changed in the last one week. The change is within me – I am now seeing him through a different set of lenses.

I ask him how he is, and state my appreciation once more, for doing this walk with me in the morning.

I am relieved to hear the energy in his voice. He, in his cheerful voice, exclaims, 'Well, I'm glad I'm doing some good for someone! And I think what I'm doing now, is what I needed back then – but didn't have. And why should I deny someone this opportunity? Especially when that person is so open to learning from a rambling older man?', he laughs.

'Roy, we all need a mentor, someone who can share their life lessons with. So we can learn vicariously from the experiences of a person whose life is different and sometimes from an era different to ours. We have the prospect of experiencing a time that we would have never been able to live in; to learn from the wisdom and wealth of knowledge of another person's life. It's always good to crystallize these pearls of wisdom', he explains.

I am overwhelmed, and tell him, 'I just don't have the words to describe how grateful I am...'

He nods in return. 'I guess it's easy for me to explain things using my life Roy. So that's what I will do. But it is not a recipe or a prescription for how it should be. It is just an experience and that's where it will stop'.

We walk in silence for a minute, listening only to the waves crashing on to the beach. And then Ed takes a deep breath and starts to narrate his story.

'So, to pick up from where we stopped Roy... It wasn't easy coming back to a place I had left long ago with no expectations of returning for good. It wasn't easy coming back to nothing career-wise, finance-wise. It was tough, you see. It was really tough'.

'Both my wife and I had left the country so long ago and we didn't have many close friends. My wife, through the few connections she had, tried to connect me with many people. But the thing was, I was not sure what I wanted to do in the first place. I couldn't get around to even thinking about it', he reflects.

Ed continues, 'But I am someone who likes to see myself as a realist, so usually, if I know something has gone wrong, I am someone who would confront it and rectify it'.

We walked in silence for a while. Ed begins again in his pensive mood, 'I knew that the longer I waited, the more it would affect my family. During that time Roy, there was a 180-degree flip in my priorities. My family became my number one. It was my father-in-law; he was a real star in this journey of mine. I expected to be judged and ridiculed, particularly by family. But he treated me with honour. He said to me that what was happening in my life was just that – life itself! He asked me not to read too much into things; he said I should focus on doing what I can do with what I have, and not focus on what I had missed out'.

Ed smiles as he speaks, 'He would visit us frequently. He would say that my wife bakes the best butter cakes, and would call in the morning to check whether I was in and he would come home, to that two-bedroomed annex. He walked with me through that time. He probably didn't understand everything I said; he probably could not empathize with my ambitions. But he still walked with me anyway. And for me, this was a great strength; a man in his mid-eighties, walking with me, talking about life, failure, and what true victory was'.

'He defined true victory as transcendence from adverse circumstances', Ed says. 'He said victory was about seeing beyond what was happening now – rising above the ashes, to know that things were happening behind the scenes and the idea was to focus on preparation for the long haul rather than on short term gain. And if not for those weeks and weeks of walking side by side with my father in law, I would not have been able to bounce back the way I did'.

Ed stops for a moment. I wait patiently.

'So, this mentoring is something I value a lot. I used it in my organization later. My father-in-law had been a secretary to certain influential lawyers in the country; he was a humble, down-to-earth man. It had been three months since I returned, and one day, he asked me, if I would like to do something different. He spoke of a lawyer who had a family business in manufacturing, with some product lines booming while certain others nearing bankruptcy. He needed someone trustworthy to support him. My father in law insisted that my perfectionism would be helpful to this lawyer', Ed recalls.

'So I went for the interview and I got the job. Initially, I was managing just one factory. And I was doing fine. I had to get used to things, acclimatize myself to the business world, which is quite different from the medical world. In the world of a doctor you are treated with prestige and you are in certain instances almost godlike. But in the business world, you are just another person, if I may say so', Ed says smilingly.

'My strategic thinking for business plans and models that envision the future and map the pathway in a step-by-step process, came in handy. I am a conceptual guy so I was happy to put structures in place while maintaining a sense of flexibility to suit the transition from a close-knit family business to a professional entity. The culture was different; what motivated people, what ticked them on, were all different. I did what I had to do, but of course, it took a few months for me to become fully comfortable in that setting; to accept who I was now: a total disruption of identity. In my heart, I was a doctor and it was difficult to erase that', Ed admits.

'You know, my father-in-law lived up to the age of 95, and he passed away only a few months ago. Those last ten years of his life, it felt almost as if he lived for me. It sounds so bizarre. But I know, that it was his encouragement and mere presence that made me want to try and persist. He shared stories of characters from his childhood and his parents and grandparents. He was able to connect me with a bygone era of world wars and depressions. He became the father I never had. My own father had died when I was two and I have no memory of him whatsoever, except for one photo on the day of my first birthday', Ed tells me.

I reflect and think to myself how similar the storyline is, the only difference being that I remember my father very well, and that he passed away when I was fourteen.

Ed continues, 'A mentor is like a spine – the spine that helps you with stability and balance. It helps you stand straight and keeps you confident. The spine that helps you walk and hold the body and all its organs in shape. For me during those times, if I had not had my father-in-law holding my bones in space, the spine in my life, I doubt that I would have been able to turn things around in life the way I did'.

Ed's voice is sincere as he reminisces, 'He didn't turn things around for me – I did that myself, but he was there to hold that space in time for me so I could be myself, reflect, learn, experiment, and make mistakes. And even though I did not realize it then, it meant a lot'.

Once again, I feel overwhelmed by the candid, honest account of Ed's experiences. I feel touched by the sense of gratitude he emanates as he talks about his experiences – the glow that radiates as he speaks about his father in law.

'So, when I realized it, I started doing this for the people who worked for me in the organizations, young and old managers alike. I mentored my teams in the organization, the CEO and the Heads of Departments. I was the sounding board, the advisor, the story-teller sharing stories openly from my days in the operating room, always hoping these experiences would be of value to those around me. And that was what helped me make these organizations become successful, the give-and-take from past and present and envisaging a future together for someone else', he stops for a while to check whether I have any questions, and begins again.

'At the same time, I didn't want to sacrifice too much time working. I was clear about this when I joined the second venture under the same owner. I told them, their money was well spent if they allocated more time out of my job description to mentor teams. And that's what the management did. Did they see results? Yes they did. The companies that were almost about to close due to union action reopened with a new sense of vigour;

people who were on strike came back to work. I worked with the union leaders and convinced them to look at the same issues from another perspective', Ed smiles with pride.

'Wow', I almost whisper under my breath.

Ed continues, 'It takes so much commitment. I would take these guys out; I would take them to a place where I could talk to them openly about what's important to them. You can't mentor people in a toxic environment. You can't talk about someone's career path and assure them that the company wants them to grow personally, when you know in reality, that there are people at the top who want to crush their dreams'.

'My next assignment was to change this toxic culture with the management and middle management. When I meet you next week Roy, I will talk about that. That was the hardest. Harder than running a clinic or being a surgeon', Ed comments laughingly.

'People start to make decisions that are best for themselves and the company, when the company is truly concerned about their growth. Some left and most of them are still in touch with me. They made some informed choices for themselves and they are doing fairly well. One person, in fact, took a year off to start a small group that helps fishermen manage finances and helps them with strategies that can help plan for the long-term. Another took a job in a completely different field in agriculture; one he was passionate about but had previously postponed working on. Then there was this lady who set out to start her own business in connecting the SMEs with possible investors and buyers. And the one I love most is a guy almost my age, taking an early retirement to go back to becoming a science teacher in a school', Ed recounts.

'You see Roy these guys were not necessarily well off when they made those decisions. They still had families to look after and children who depended on them. They just made sure that they found a way to do both in such a way their happiness was not always compromised', Ed comments wisely.

I am intrigued. Curious, I ask 'How did the organization take it? Your mentoring would have resulted in people realizing that they were in the wrong place. If the organizations had invested on them, the management wouldn't have been happy'.

Ed nods to my question, 'Ah, good question. Now that is the mindset I had to change in the management. If a person is not happy and has a better plan for himself, you are better off letting him go despite the investment you have made in his growth in the past. You see, it was not even five percent of the people I mentored who left. The others, more or less thrived and we were able to identify where they would fit in best in the organization. We shuffled and restructured according to their strengths'.

'Didn't you face resistance?', I ask, startled by his approach.

Ed nods again and answers, 'Of course I did. Resistance is very natural. It can happen to you and me. I was direct; being straightforward, honest and open matters most. I set up a confidential grievance- handling team supervised by me. They had to record all the issues for me to evaluate the pulse of the people. I was available to answer their questions anytime. We worked on enriching the jobs with tasks that resonated with them intrinsically; things they were good at and liked to do, whether it was organizing events, internal training or knowledge sharing sessions, or being a buddy in hand-holding the new recruits. We worked on job rotations, to make them multi-skilled; this also increased the level of appreciation as people began to see the connections amongst the teams, and how holistically they became one. They came to realize their contribution to the bigger picture, the larger vision'.

Sensing my skepticism in all this, he continues, 'You see Roy, many people invest in the top 20 percent of the company, the cream of the cream and they are developed to make great advances in their careers. But I believe in the remaining eighty per cent, the so called middle band or lower band, even in some cases the so called 'dead wood'. I tried to find out one or two variables that would increase the work satisfaction that translated into productivity by at least ten percent of this bottom eighty percent'.

'Guess what happened: the results were phenomenal. They felt valued and they started to give an extra five to ten per cent more; that increase is huge when you consider 80 per cent of your people contributing', he says.

'Wow', I utter, in awe. 'So what were these variables?' I ask.

Ed replies, 'They were different for different teams, and also where they were in the hierarchy was an important aspect. For the bottom most level, it was more or less working hours, pay, and good leadership from the supervisors. But as it went up the hierarchy, it was about appreciation and finding a sense of purpose, not necessarily in that job alone, but in life overall'.

'You see, if we don't address this sense of purpose overall in life, we are left with nothing to reason out why we are stuck in a particular place at a particular time. I tried to show them how working in this company at this stage in their life could be aligned to their overall life purpose. And whenever there was misalignment, I encouraged them to leave – because it was the right thing to do', he explains.

'I have to be honest – I was more on the people's side, than on the organization's', Ed admits. 'But being on the people's side helped in the growth of the company. People came to work because they knew *why* they were coming through those doors to work at the machines every day. Why they were in an assembly line, why they had to work as a team, why achieving targets together was important. I identified people who were motivators within these teams, and I especially spent time to mentor them so that they can lead by example'.

'Wow', I say, again. 'That's a rare case study!' I add.

'I don't take much credit Roy. These were basic observations that I made as an outsider, new to the corporate world. I never knew how much I loved people until I started doing this job. I loved to hear their success stories and I am honored to have been a part of their decision making journey. To date, even if I don't hear from them, I am still happy to have invested on them. The change and success is theirs to enjoy', Ed says concluding.

I ask, 'Many people who mentor, share their stories and expect that the lessons they learnt or the way they did things to be still relevant to another person. I find this to be a bit one-sided and asymmetrical as the other person's situation could be very different'.

'Yes, that thinking is not right. If not done keeping the other person in mind, it can be a good ego-trip to the mentor, to feel important. Sometimes, we derive a sense of identity of self-importance when people come to us and flock around us for advice. This is not mentoring. Any lesson of maturity has to be contextualized to the person receiving it. And mentoring is also about drawing the voice out of the person, so that the person himself understands and relates to these lessons of maturity', Ed explains.

'So, it is not telling but providing enough for the person to stand on, so the person will be able to see the relevance?', I ask inquiringly.

'Yes, and also to find their own voice in their own decisions; and as I mentioned before, to hold someone in that space in time so they can be who they are', Ed adds further.

A train approaches from the South, commanding our attention.

'Now look at that beauty!', Ed stops to observe. 'Ok Roy, time for me to walk alone now. I will see you next week'.

'Yes Ed. that sounds good. Thank you again', I say.

'Take care', Ed smiles widely and starts to walk faster as I decide to head back home.

While walking, I see two trains on their paths; they travel close yet they travel in parallel just for a short time before they head in their opposite directions.

The sleepy gulls spread their wings over the mild dawn of the skies.

I suddenly feel poetic and I smile to myself. 'To hold someone in that space in time so they can be who they are': I like that very much!

....

Back at work

I start compiling the concerns and needs of the people for me to communicate to my manager who will be back after his visit to the US the next day. I receive some threatening anonymous calls pressurizing me to make the process clearer and to get the top managers to communicate this more clearly and directly, rather than leaving room for regret. I try to think who would be behind this as I have spoken to everyone in person and have established a sense of understanding.

They tell me I am heartless to be a part of this, knowing so well that ultimately everyone will be sent home. They call me a 'shameful sucker' and say that I will have to pay one day for what I am doing to the people.

Finally, I am able to connect with my boss over the phone and I start relating the happenings. He says to continue what I am doing, and that he would meet me over a drink in the evening. I tell him that I don't want the drink, and that I really need more information and assistance to pursue this. I tell him that it is our responsibility to ensure that we minimize the uncertainty even though some form of it will always be unavoidable. He seems annoyed with me for some reason, and as usual hangs up saying that he is getting another call.

More and more, I feel as if I am the bait, the pawn, and that makes me very, very angry. I tell this to my wife who advices me to speak to another director from a different division or even the GM of the plant. Why is everyone so cold and washing their hands off this? It is true that the GM and the HR are aware of this initiative but why are they not there to support me?

One morning, I open my inbox to find a sector-wide email attached with a series of pictures of my ex-girlfriend from university and I shabbily patched and merged together. It is obvious that it is a job of a novice and in my anger I mutter to myself, 'Whoever you are, learn how to con properly or don't con at all.'

I call Naren and tell him, 'Let me send whoever to a good graphic design class man. I'll personally sponsor it'.

Naren answers with a laugh, but goes to say that my wife is also copied in the email. I hit the roof.

In a frenzy, I grab the findings from the one-to-one conversations and run towards the GMs office. I crash into his office, visibly flustered, but he only looks up and goes back to what he is reading.

'Please I need someone here to support me...why is no one talking to me or explaining things to me?', I demand.

'It is your boss's project and I cannot be answerable to this. I have very little information. Your boss, who claims to have received a directive from the very top, wants to experiment on this and see. If it works it's great and maybe it will be replicated in other plants', the GM says, only granting me an impassive glance as he continues reading.

'But if it doesn't?' I ask exasperatedly.

'Well, you can ask your boss', he snaps.

'This is unfair. I have worked with you for longer and the least you can do is to let me know what is really happening. Why is everyone so quiet?', I demand.

'Roy, I have a conference call now. Please talk to your boss about this', he gestures that I leave.

'No, you can't ask me to leave. You are the head of this plant and you should know what is happening', I retort.

'Roy, I am telling you', he tells me, looking me in the eye. 'I know very little about this. Your boss is highly connected in this organization. It is best if everyone minds their own business'. He goes back to looking at his screen.

'Yes, except for me who is left with no one to turn to. I actually don't care about my job but I care about these people. Seriously... what sort of an organization am I working for?', I demand in angst.

'You have to leave now Roy, please', he mutters, without looking at me.

I stare at him for a few seconds and leave, shutting the door loudly behind me. People at office look up from their desks questioningly.

Seriously! They should all mind their own business then!

I am so angry that I feel the grinding of my teeth, the pounding of my heart and the rush of blood in my head, taking me to the limit one more time!

I inform my wife about the pictures before she gets to open her email and explain what is happening on the work-front today. I was surprised to hear her voice calm and contained when she asks me not to waste time to investigate who is behind it, but to focus my energy to get the findings across to the sector CEO in the absence of any support from the factory.

....

BRAIN FOR THY THOUGHT

I meet Ed on Saturday morning. Our conversations have become so intense that for me, as strange as it may sound, it has almost been therapeutic to be able to listen to someone whose journey had been much more difficult than mine. And here I am, so daunted by something happening in my own organization. But when I look at Ed's life, I realize that this man may have had some enormous agility to have been able to adapt and fight the resistance to change. I feel that if he was able to make that huge transition from being a medical doctor to an organizational leader, I could aspire for some success too, in my challenge at work.

These meetings have been of some encouragement to me, and I guess Ed has been like a spine, supporting me through it all. So as I meet him today, I'm really curious to know more about what happened in his organization. Ed was, after all, someone who had to change a leadership culture, influencing those at the top who may have created a toxic environment, smothering people with their insecurities, while all the while boasting to the outside world about the brilliance of their leadership. Well this is not a unique scenario, it's way too common in the organizational world.

When I mention it, Ed laughs at my enthusiasm. 'Ha! Roy, Roy – I've been keeping you up I guess? You've been thinking about this way too much. Tell me, how is your wife and how are the kids?'

'Oh they're fine Ed. My wife is particularly resilient given what has been happening at work', I answer with a sense of appreciation.

'And the kids? How old are they again?', Ed asks.

'My daughter is four, and my son is six months', I reply.

'Interesting times! Roy, never forget, that's your priority. That's your first responsibility. They need you and you need them. Never doubt that', he adds.

'Yes Ed, I know', I reply, smiling at his serious tone.

'So, where were we?', he asks.

'You were speaking about the company's leadership and how you changed them', I prompt.

'Yeah. So, it was a manufacturing organization, and when the owner saw what I was capable of doing, not because I wanted to prove a point, but for some reason I was actually good at it, he said to me that if I stick around with the company for another 3 years, he would acquire many more businesses, but I would have to act as his corner man', Ed recounts.

'Anyway, he said he needed my brains. And I asked him what that meant. This was a man, a third generation businessman who had made it so big in the corporate world; and he wanted my brains? A medical brain at that?', Ed laughs. 'Well, I said, if it's something I could do without compromising much on my family front, I would be happy to do it'.

'All this time I wasn't sure if I was doing the right thing with my life. By profession a doctor, and by default a corporate leader now. The point is, I was uncertain of who I was. Forty-four years old, still not sure, with a scattered identity. This was beyond mid-life crisis!', Ed asserts.

'One thing was for sure, the more I worked, the more I saw, and the more I saw, the more I was convinced I was doing something right. Just to balance things off, I met a friend from school, who was a pilot but who also headed his own NGO. I volunteered to help him at his NGO. It brought some balance, and I felt being available to a worthy cause opened my eyes to the areas in society that we can miss very easily in the rush of this rat race. It's a local NGO, a small one that does some real work. Sometimes or most of the time, it's the people who don't talk much who end up doing a lot. It's the same in the organizations as well Roy!', Ed laughs.

'My biggest challenge at work was that they had twelve companies and four sons in charge of these different companies; as they were all family owned, the companies had unique cultures and sub-cultures that made matters worse. Some of these companies were so embedded in their family values, and more often than not, rotated around one person, who would give much responsibility, but not the power and authority for people to carry out the duties', Ed explains.

'There was no formal process that was transparent for people to understand. The power structure was so centralized at the top and you find the friends and family of these sons acting almost like bodyguards to the owners. People would suck up to them and filter information only to say the right thing so they could be in the good books of the sons', he adds.

Ed continues, 'Worse still was when the extended family and relations who were working there brought in their family disputes and disagreements to the management meetings. It was chaos and the father, who was the main shareholder, who was now eighty-five years old, was still signing cheques and making decisions on even very small issues such as whether someone should go on their annual leave or not. Some were unconsciously so possessive of power. I don't blame them; they had built a successful brand, but sustaining it in this day and age was questionable', he reflects.

'So each and every company had to be evaluated in terms of the big guy and his four sons who by the way had very different working and leadership styles. It had to be further studied keeping in mind the employee demographics from the different geographical areas of the companies and factories, how it made business-sense as some brands were doing better than the others', Ed says.

'It took me about a good year to be able to work on this. It was not about giving third party advice here; it was about going there, eating with the people, breathing the same air and occupying the same space. It was important to build a connection, to help them understand you, and for you to understand them –to relate to some of the values within these separate entities. And that's what I did. Once again, I was away from my family, but this time I made an effort to spend time with them regardless', he adds.

'I used to work in different locations, different factories, and come home during the weekends. Recreating these cultures that were so unique to each and every organization wasn't easy. One of the things I discovered about myself as a doctor, was that I liked to work alone as a specialist even though in reality you work as a team in the theatre. But as a specialist surgeon, I have a set of skills I can procedurally and consistently use to excel in my own work', Ed adds smilingly.

He continues, 'But working with people is more complicated; humans are unpredictable, and the dynamics within a team are so different to a team of nurses or doctors you work with when you have to, and anyway these are temporary teams. Right now, between you and me, the dynamic is simpler and we both understand it. But the moment we add your wife, my wife, our children, and other people to the equation, this dynamic changes. Others' mere presence changes the interaction between us. I had to understand that. And for some reason I was able to understand how some variable dynamics act as a catalyst to moderate some of the intense tensions that can hinder certain teams, especially management teams'.

'A lot of people talk about leadership; how many books are there?' Ed asks. 'Countless! Sometimes I wonder if it's something we can capture to begin with. Leadership gurus, numerous MBA programs, management schools, they all attempt to crystallize leadership, but I really doubt that you could ever capture the wholeness of leadership in just one formula'.

He continues to add, 'In my experience, leadership is to be devoid of a desire to shine just as you are. So, for example, there is no "me" in leadership. If you try to work on things based on this "me", you lose the plot. Leadership which is more about "WE" or "US", is becoming more and more difficult because everything is about 'me, myself and I' these days. To lead is to bring everyone, including yourself to the same purpose, be it a family, a team, a company, or a community'.

Thoughtfully, Ed continues, 'I felt sorry for the father, the big guy; you know at that age you would not want to carry the burden of all this. He was worried and had no confidence in his sons to sustain the companies. He questioned his own sense of leadership over his sons throughout the years. I told him that anyone can be a great leader in a system where everything is perfect, where everyone is doing what they are expected to, etc. But great leadership is one that takes control during chaos, when you can put things in order when things aren't going right, when you can see some sort of pattern in the crisis and get people to move in one direction despite obstacles and resistance'.

'I said to him that he could decide who he can delegate some of his work to and maybe letting go is not such a bad idea given his constant admittance to the hospital for palpitations. It took him a while but after he carefully observed me over eight months, he asked me to give him a master plan of how I intended to approach the project in every factory. Now, that was tough and it took three months for me to convince him that this plan was plausible', Ed reflects.

Suddenly, his face lights up with a wide grin. 'That's when the RockStars Project was launched'.

'Why RockStars?', I ask curiously, smiling to myself.

Ed responds with a grin, 'Ah! Hold your horses boy. RockStars were the ones to lead by setting an example, and I'm telling you now: Leadership requires a lot of character. And as the big guy said, you need brains. Yes, you need brains to lead. But what is required even more is character. And people just don't get it! Seriously Roy, we don't get it. I have nothing against people going to learn leadership – it's important that people learn and educate themselves. But you see, look at that fishing boat Roy. Those guys go to the ocean almost every day. Is the ocean predicable? No. Do they even know whether they're going to get what they're after? No. Are the conditions ideal? No', Ed stops.

I turn to look at the nearest fishermen's boat, which is being pushed off the shore to the shallow waters until it is afloat in sufficiently deep water. The ocean is calm this morning, and the sky seems clear. But Ed is right, it could change in the blink of an eye.

Echoing my thoughts, Ed continues, 'The fishermen who bring us the fish we eat, face some of the worst work environments. I feel we've got it all wrong. Why are the fishermen able to survive in this country, in this coastal belt? Is it because the technology is great or the boat is solid and sturdy? Yes, these are contributors, but there is always something that continues to remain uncertain in the sea. There's one thing that defines them that makes it possible for them to continue in the job, and that is fearlessness. They go against the tide. Leaders do that too'.

'RockStars focus on growth. When you do weights Roy, you apply a tremendous amount of stress to the muscles. To withstand the force and to make the stress more bearable the bone grows and remodels to increase the surface area. Especially after bone injury, applying specific stress in particular directions to the bone can help it become normal healthy bone again. I used this principle to increase the need to change within these companies. I told these selected RockStars that they need to see the changes that were coming, (which they saw as adversity), as an opportunity to grow and increase capacity in character', Ed explains proudly.

He continues, 'RockStars use their brains; I thought about this the day my CEO told me about needing my brains. It's funny, I as a doctor, when I think of organs with my knowledge and love of the human anatomy, I can see so many parallels and draw so many metaphors from this. I thought the brain was synonymous with the leader or the head of the company. You've got to be able to make the right decisions with a blend of logic and rationality. You've got to be able to strategize. You've got to be able to see a vision your people may not be able to see. You might be summoned to war overnight. You need to have made the right decisions about sharpening your tools or training the armies for the battles. Yes, you need the brains', he smiles looking at me.

I smile back at his enthusiasm. Such a refreshing spirit!

'Many companies or even countries are brain-dead today', Ed comments wisely. 'Or terribly ill in the mind. They can't think straight. They don't make the tough call even when they know it is the right thing to do. There's a leadership vacuum. A huge one! It's everywhere in the world. Look at the governments today! People who are not fit in their mind to lead – are leading anyway'.

After a few moments of reflection, I comment, 'The problem with leadership is that it comes with so much societal glamour, you know, it's great to be featured in Fortune 500. To be one among the other tycoons who are exalted in these features. And in these articles, people are glorified for what they have done, but no one ever talks about the difficulties faced in getting there'.

I continue, 'These days, the latest hype is about entrepreneurs. Everyone wants to be an entrepreneur; it's hip and trendy. However, no one realizes that many a common man is an entrepreneur when he manages a shop in the community, and mind you, this isn't an esteemed position to have. But now, it's a fashionable word. There's this constant coupling of the term entrepreneurship with greatness, courage and bravery. Even the most simple journey is so sensationalized that some think that they need a sort of humble beginning to boast about the greatness of their achievement', I laugh.

Ed responds laughing out loud, 'Oh, I've seen enough of this tom-foolery! All these stories carefully crafted through techniques of story-telling to applaud themselves and boast how great they are'.

Ed further adds, 'Yes indeed I have noticed that. If one is not willing to let go of this 'me, myself and I' concept, if one is not willing to reflect the credit back on the people who actually do the work, if one is not willing to receive feedback and look at things from a different perspective so they see the bigger picture, then one should not take up responsibility to begin with. Humility is a primary qualifier for leadership'.

He continues, 'Another thing, some leaders forget that we human beings have this incredible ability to be able to read what's genuine and what's fake. Sometimes in the glorious words, flair, and the gift of the gab that people use in their leadership and management styles, the followers can get lost, and people call them charismatic leaders'.

I add, 'What use does charisma have if you are not using it the right way? Charisma can also be very dangerous. And throughout history we have examples of leaders who've used charisma in right and wrong ways, and the wrong way always had very destructive consequences! Charisma is not leadership; it is almost a personality trait. In fact, there are many leaders who have no charisma, and do so much work and are quiet and humble about it'.

We walk in silence. It is still quite dark.

I ask impatiently, 'Still, why RockStars? They could be famous, having a fan club and all that jazz. Some could be good in what they do but not all. They could be trendsetters but does the trend always serve a purpose?' I laugh.

'And they can be addicts too, so one can't necessarily say they set an example', I further add as an afterthought.

Ed smiles at me, 'Ha! Roy', he says, pointing to Venus in the dark morning skies. 'What is that?'

Amused, I reply, 'Venus, the planet'.

'How do you think the earth looks like from outer space?', he asks suddenly.

'Somewhat like Venus I guess', I muse.

'Yes, so a bright planet like that rock star?', he asks pointing to Venus again.

'Ah. Yes', I acquiesce smiling. 'Clever'.

Ed explains, 'Our rock star, the earth, knows its perfect place in the system, neither too hot nor too cold. It is aligned with the rest of the planets and respects the interconnections. It is disciplined enough to stick to its orbit and is consistent in its pace. It does not have light of its own but only reflects the light of the super star the life-giver of the system but is willing to mother a unique life-force within. It is so resilient, with an in-built regulatory system to manage the harmful effects of our own actions that challenge its balance. From the glaciers to volcanoes, from great oceans to vast continents, from a rain drop to the lakes of the land, from a grain of sand to majestic mountains, the trees and flowers, the fruits, the animals, and the birds of all the forests to the fish in the seven seas, our rock star knows them all, bears them all, nourishes them all'.

'And loves them all... How beautiful!', I complete, smiling.

'The perfect rock star, the perfect leader in the system ahead of the curve', he laughs.

I laugh and ask him inquisitively, 'Where on earth do you get these analogies from?'

'From Earth Roy, from Earth itself'.

We both laugh before he says, 'Give credit to Lucas my son. He tends to ask the right questions when I need the inspiration.'

We walk in silence and I feel I am ready to face the day.

He turns to me, and says kindly, 'I know Roy that your work situation isn't ideal right now. But people trust you. Some may react out of fear but a majority of people trust you because there is something about you that shows genuineness and sincerity. People also see that you've been given a very difficult task to do. So tell me, how will you use that to do good to those people and the organization?'

He pauses, allowing me to ponder on this, and then adds, 'Doing good to the organization, and good by the people – these have to be on the same side of the scale. By being good to the people if you are failing your management, or by being on the management's side if you're failing the people; either way it is a win-lose scenario. In this case, you will have to weigh your costs of quitting or continuing in a job where your values are in misalignment with what is required of you. It's as simple as that'.

Simple? I look at him in surprise, and he holds my gaze with a serious look in his eyes.

'You've been given a job. But you won't do any wrong given your principles. Am I right?', he asks.

'Yes, Ed', I reply. 'I just need to see that I'm capable of doing good to both the company and its people at the same time'.

'Roy, don't get me wrong. But weeding is required within us anyway. We need to get rid of our own internal weeds that do not serve us well. We need to get rid of the weeds in our families; the things we aren't doing right, the erratic patterns and habits', Ed advises.

'In organizations, we need to remove the weeds, lest it devour the garden. I had to communicate such bad news to many people in those companies Roy, some from the extended family of the owners and that wasn't pleasant. What if we look at the betterment of the whole? As long as termination is the last resort, after giving them an opportunity and adequate time to change in a safe environment first, weeding is not a bad thing and in fact might be the best thing that can happen to people who have been asked to leave', Ed concludes.

'Yup, that's what my proposal is about Ed, the next six months are crucial', I tell him, smiling.

'That's great. Now go implement it', Ed responds.

'It's that easy!' I comment, smiling almost sarcastically.

'The thought of quitting has crossed my mind', I admit.

'I know, but nothing comes easy. How many people are involved in this operation, now?', he questions.

'The factory total?', I ask.

'Yes', he clarifies.

'Four thousand'.

'Great. If you quit, you give up on those four thousand lives. Even the people who will ultimately have to go, will appreciate it if you invest enough time to help them plan their future. Two of my most dedicated RockStars personally did that with people I had to let go of. Go and inject some fearlessness. You have tremendous potential to bring about a new and better equilibrium within the company and you will only know it if you do it', he encourages.

'What about the people I have to get rid of, in case they resist this change? People with kids, with lifestyles built on their salaries? By asking them to leave, I'm letting down entire families', my voice weakens, spelling out my fear and confusion.

'You're not just asking them to leave, are you Roy? You're giving them the opportunity to change, just like I am showing you the opportunity to change. If you don't do this, you're going to be one of those managers who resist change. Someone else would not take time like you to find the best solution. What if someone heartless replaces you?', Ed challenges me in a calm voice.

I nod in response, and focus my thoughts on the rhythmic pounding of the waves on a boat moored on the shore. The sea seems rough. I realize the enormous truth in Ed's words. If I feel for these people, I need to become the brain of this project.

Ed Interrupts, 'Now, I'm going to have some *pol sambol* and *rotti*. I will see you in a week's time Roy!'. With these parting words, Ed walks away to cross the rail tracks.

....

Back at work

My boss walks in the next day and asks me to come to his office. He asks me what has been happening.

I tell him that I find it difficult to work with no support and little information. I tell him how people have started to attack my personal life in vengeance.

'What do you mean little information? I have told you what I know and what the Board has asked me to do', he demands.

I sit down and take a deep breath, and place the findings from the one-to-ones. I tell him that I want him to go through the findings, and that it is necessary to ensure that the managers' collective voice has been heard by the people who commissioned this initiative before making any decision about them. I tell him that he needs to talk to them directly, that they would take him more seriously and that they will not feel devalued. I tell him that we have a responsibility to preserve and protect the self-worth of the people.

'Roy, what did I tell you the day I gave you this assignment? I have faith in you to implement it. They have to see you as someone who has the authority to carry this out', he insists.

I ask him why my role was never formally announced to the factory, to which he does not answer. I ask him again to write an email to all the selected managers copying me to explain the process. He says he will do it before the end of the day.

'What else do you want me to do? How else can I support you?', he asks. I get irritated by his false promises and fake attitude of support.

'Please read these concerns that they have mentioned. I have made an easy-to-read document for you. I also analyzed and graphed the numbers of the survey so that it's all there in a snap shot. Can I explain this to you now?', I ask him not trusting him to read it.

'No I will read it quietly before writing that email. Go get all their salary details from HR and ask someone from HR to come see me,' he orders. I don't trust this guy anymore. I get a bad feeling about all this; there is something else here that I cannot see.

The mobile that is on his table starts to ring.

From the corner of my eye, I notice that the caller is the GM of the plant.

Even though I desperately want to stay now, he waves implying that I leave.

Back in the HR department, people are cynical towards me and ignore my requests saying that they are busy and are getting ready for the audits tomorrow.

I go to the HR Director and request the salary particulars from him.

He smiles from the corner of this mouth. 'Oh! So now you come for help? Why not before?', he asks scathingly.

'I asked whether we could do this collaboratively, but no one was interested', I defend myself.

'Not interested?', he asks, raising his eyebrows.

'Yes, I have come here several times and you know it because you have seen me. One day, one of your assistant managers asked me why I was wasting time here', I reply.

'Please don't carry tales around here', he accuses.

'I am not. I am telling you that I tried to work with your team and that no one cared two hoots about it, even though it should have been a corporative effort', I react, clearly agitated. I become conscious of my tone of voice.

'You wanted our help when you felt abandoned by your boss, and I thought your boss made it very clear to you that you would be alone from the beginning', he retorts, probably giving me more rope to hang from.

'Please, I need those salary details', I almost plead.

'We don't divulge such confidential information to anyone. It's our policy', he says with an air of importance.

I grab a seat and look at him, totally worn out and almost ready to give up.

'What's really happening?', I ask in a hushed voice, struggling to keep my voice from sounding pleading again.

'You tell me Roy? Aren't you the change champion here?', he challenges.

I remain quiet for sometime before leaving his office.

As I approach my boss' office I notice my colleague, Naren from his desk gesturing wildly at his phone, indicating that I should check my phone. Sure enough, I see a message from him, reading 'This guy is crazy. Be careful of what you say'.

I nod to indicate that I got the message.

I tap on the door and enter. I find my boss puffing away a cigarette with the window partially open, even though the air-conditioning is on.

'Sit down Roy', his voice is curt.

I grab a chair and sit down.

'What is this nonsense? This is not what I want, all this mushy stuff! Do you think this is what brings money to a company? Do you think that this is what I asked you to do in the first place? I wanted you to communicate to them clearly that they will have to go home if they don't change their game plan. Clearly you are not doing your job properly; look at my inbox and these threat emails! It looks like my FB page is hacked too', he says with fury.

Ah! Serves him right!

'I did what I can with the limited information I had', I reply.

Secretly, it feels justified; taste of his own medicine.

'Really, whoever selected you for the succession plan was not in his right mind when he did that', he almost screams.

I breathe, and breathe again and again to notice the gap between what he just said and what my response could be. Keeping myself in check, I say as calmly as I can, 'You took me out of my career plan and asked me to do this Boss'.

'Yes, because I thought you were competent,' he shouts.

I keep quiet.

He continues, 'What rubbish is this? Do you think anyone cares about how people really 'feel' in an organization? Can you do anything about it even if you know? There is politics everywhere, there is gossip everywhere, dissatisfaction, and unmet expectations. You can't make everyone happy. This is a business organization. Let them leave right now, if they are not happy. Now do me a favour, destroy all the information related to these one-to-ones', he says, looking away and lighting a cigarette.

'Why? The management has the right to know', I defend.

'Don't talk about rights with me', he threatens.

At that moment, I realize that I need to keep quiet. But I wanted to ask one more thing before leaving his office. The report presents problem areas as perceived by our managers, and one whole section in the report is dedicated to perceptions on the support given by the top-management.

I alert him that more than eighty per cent of the group had complained regarding the management style of the people above them. He says that he doesn't want to hear any more and asks me to leave immediately.

Frustrated, I go back to my desk to realize that my laptop is missing, and that the printouts of the document are with the Boss. I remember how I have also not emailed it to myself, nor saved it to a common drive due to the sensitivity of the project. Devastated, and with a sinking feeling I realize I have nothing to support the concerns raised at the one-to-one chats.

Completely disturbed by this, I sweep the files off my desk in anger. I sit down, defeated, to see my phone light up with an incoming message.

Naren, again.

Dreading the possibility that I might be disappointing him too, I open the message.

I read, 'It's the final countdown man: Don't be stupid. I have your back'.

A wave of relief gushes through me. I smile with gratitude; what a killer player Naren is!

....

MOUTH FOR THY PITCH

It is Saturday and I am waiting to meet Ed, once again. It is as if I am on a fast-track development plan that requires me to go for classes so often. I love these chats, and in fact it is what keeps me going.

Ed starts his morning lessons, 'Roy, over the past month or so, you've been on a journey at work that has really made you see things differently or 'forced' you to see things differently. And I hope you're proud of yourself to have accepted this challenge. Someone who was hesitant yet persevered despite the unknown and the ambiguity'.

'Yes Ed', I reply. 'But, I don't want to evaluate and think too much about it right now. Maybe after all this is over, I'll be in a place where I'm ready to reflect on that'.

'I hope you reflect on what you're doing and how you're doing things', Ed adds.

'Yes', I agree. 'I take down notes. I reflect on things I could have done differently and save it as my screen-saver till I can replace it with my next learning points. I also get my colleague to give me constant feedback on how I can improve when it comes to this project', I add, smiling.

'That's good Roy!', Ed commends.

'So, what do you have for me today?', I ask impatiently.

'Patience Roy, patience', he laughs. 'I have Mandela today'.

'Ah!', I smile. 'One of my favourites too'.

Ed nods in assent, 'He had a vision for South Africa that has been subjugated by the apartheid, to dismantle the institutionalized racism. He stood as a voice for himself and for the down-trodden, and was ready to speak up for the rights of the people. If you look at the early years of his life, you can see the number of times he got into trouble, often resulting in repeatedly being arrested. But it was the sentence he received in 1962, of being kept behind bars for life that shaped his character and molded him to be who he is remembered for'.

I nod in agreement. The story of Nelson Mandela is one I have heard multiple times over the years; each time, I reflect, I have learnt something new, or appreciate his example differently. Glancing at Ed's focused expression as he walked on, I wonder what new perspective on this hero that Ed would bring to me today.

Ed continues his narration, 'When President Klerk ordered him to be released after 27 years of imprisonment amidst pressures from the international community and fears of a civil war, Mandela was ready to embark on his mission. He walked out with a clear mission; racial reconciliation. This goal was the backdrop of his work, and it governed everything he did from that point. What do you think gave birth to this perspective?', he asks.

'Long years of isolation in the prison', I offer. 'Waiting and patience: integrity, as he walked the talk when he was released and was elected as the president in those first multi-racial elections. His voice drew people to relate to him as their own, a voice that spoke with defiance when needed, but with gentle forgiveness in his general affairs to even those who persecuted him', I add with confidence as I have read much about him.

Ed builds on what I say.

'Yes, his influence was largely based on the commitment he demonstrated to not quitting. This made him a role model; to be able to persevere, to be determined not to lose sight of the vision for his country and his people', he continues.

'The key to being influential is that you are a voice of advocacy for others. That people identify with you. There's something in you that resonates with the people and they love you for that. They don't just work for you because they like you, but because they want to follow you, and be like you because of who you are. This is how Mandela led ANC to victory in 1994', Ed reflects.

The wind howls in the background. It had rained heavily earlier in the morning. The wind was still blowing in gusts, and the sand was damp beneath our feet.

'So how does this influence relate to your human body analogy?', I ask, thinking of all the organs that now hold a different meaning to me.

'The sound created in our larynx is expressed through the mouth as speech. In other words – our voice! And it's not only speech Roy, but also song, shouting, screaming, yelling and all the other emotional undertones attached', he stops and begins again.

'Your voice is unique; even if a person can't see you, they can still recognize your voice over the phone. In the same manner, your influence is also unique and people around you will know what your voice or even your mere presence could mean in that situation', Ed explains.

He continues thoughtfully, 'You see when I think of 'voice', I often think about those days when my wife went completely quiet. She wouldn't say a word. But did that mean she didn't have much to say? No. A voice is an expression. Our own voices are our self-expressions. We can use that for our benefit alone. But what if you use your voice to win the rights/needs of many other people? And in organizations, you and I have been given that opportunity. I feel honoured to be given that opportunity'.

I find myself challenged once more, by his way of phrasing my work situation. I am happy that I have not quit so far.

Ed remains quiet. I hear the sound of the distant gulls blending with the splash of the sea, still rough after the rainstorm earlier in the day. I reflect smilingly, the crash of the waves, the howl of the wind, are like nature's voice.

'Tell me more about the voice', I ask Ed.

Nodding at my question, Ed continues, 'Knowing when to use your voice or not; knowing when to talk, when to keep quiet, and when to stop talking completely, all are equally important'.

I remember something from what I have read recently about Mandela. I add, 'Something admirable about Mandela is that he declined the second presidential term. He knew when to step down, and let his successor take over. Now, how often does that happen in the world of politics through the volition of the leader?'

He agrees with me on this, as I count several politicians from around the world that fell to defeat due to their greed for power.

'I guess Mandela spoke to people with the very voice that would have first governed his own conscience; the truth of the heart. If there had been a discrepancy between the two, we wouldn't have remembered Mandela the way we do now', I think aloud.

'Spot on! Integrity again!', Ed agrees.

It starts to drizzle and I look up to the skies, as if to refresh my view. I smell the salt in the air, and it feels heavy and saturated.

We walk in silence and the thought of a character from a story I have heard comes to mind; another prison story of a war hero who is thrown into prison for disobeying the unjustifiable commands of a king who orders the war hero to carry out a massacre against his rivals. When in prison, he sees how the prisoners are being treated inhumanely.

I narrate the story, 'The war hero who is popular amongst the citizens of the country, who has earned his titles in the army, is watched carefully by the head warden. The head warden becomes increasingly insecure by his presence as he gains respect even from the most incorrigible prisoners'.

'In order to insult the war hero, the warden instructs all the prisoners to build a wall between the two compounds in the facility within two days. Any form of break is not allowed and some prisoners are stripped naked and humiliated, made to starve or even shot dead for questioning the directives', I relate.

'It goes on to talk about how this war hero stands against the power tactics of the warden to fight for the dignity of the prisoners. It shows how he helps them to see their self-worth and focus their energy on what they can do and who they can become', I reflect.

'The story ends with the warden being shamed for his greed for power and how ultimately the prisoners are given a sense of pride for how they can make a difference in their community. With the help of another warden, the war hero gets the prisoners to develop their skills in carpentry and cookery, through which they start supplying desks for the public schools in the country and daily food for the canteens in schools and offices based around the prisons', I conclude.

As I finish the story, I silently reflect on the idea of 'Influence with integrity to fight for the vulnerable and to be a voice for the voiceless'.

Then Ed tells me, 'That's a good one Roy, very good story of influence'.

After walking in silence for a while, I recap the experience at work.

I confess finally, 'I feel like an absolute fool Ed. Everything that happened at work. This guy really had his own agenda and I was so stupid not to have seen it'.

'But Roy, you have information no one else has in the organization now. You have a great opportunity to share this with the right people', Ed suggests.

'I am not sure whether they will give me the opportunity to share this information to begin with. I would love to, as I know that will make a difference in how we do work and treat our people', I sigh.

We walk a few more lengths quietly before I ask, 'All in all, I sometimes wonder what the purpose of this whole experience is, whether it is a waste of time and resources, and as for me, whether the worst of me has come out'.

Ed looks at me carefully and responds, 'For you, it's been a journey towards character. An uphill battle, a tough one. But this journey is going to end, and you will be at a different elevation from where you can see things from a different perspective. Win or lose, you will know that you did your best. It is an experience and a learning that will prepare you for your next adventure'.

I wish it was easier though; the after-taste of the sense of failure is something that we can all do without. The sound of the rough waves amplifies in my ears. As we walk back in silence I am filled with a sense of calm even though I know that there is still much to be resolved at work.

....

Back at work

I know from my previous encounter with the boss, that from now on, it will be a one-man-show. I have to take responsibility for being naïve; I realize how fortunate it was that my colleague Naren had managed to save a copy of my report, based on a gut feeling that my computer may go missing one of these days. He laughingly tells me that such individuals more often than not, are way too predictable.

Without my knowing, Naren had also spoken to the GM and HR, and explained the situation from a third person's point of view. This had done wonders.

That evening, we were all to meet outside office to see how we could take it forward.

Amazingly, I find the GM and the HR Manager to be on my side, and they say that they couldn't intervene earlier before the situation was reported to the high ups and the required directives were obtained for damage control.

I take what they say with a pinch of salt. For the time being, it's once bitten, twice shy.

Furthermore, they tell me that more resistance is being seen from the subordinates of the target manager pool than from the managers themselves. This surprises me given what they mentioned at the focus group discussions about their managers' directive and insensitive leadership styles. There has been some rumor within this level, that part of this factory would be closed down, and that their jobs in turn would be at risk. The GM also suspects that the amateur Photoshop job was a result of defiance from this level.

They say that after the one-to-ones, they had not received a single complaint, and that people were being more proactive about wanting their development plan and the required timelines, so that they could start working on it. Some had specifically mentioned my name, and said that the chat allowed them to clear most of their doubts and explore options that they never thought existed.

What I had not envisaged was that the uncertainty would seep into the lower levels; those who are now feeling insecure about their own jobs. The HR team asks me to show all the documents and the survey statistics I have compiled, and requests me to be ready to address the managers and the entire division the moment they inform me. They also ask me to deactivate my social media accounts and to be very careful about who I speak to, for the time being.

'This is all in a day's work Roy; you are a star,' says Naren.

I wink and respond, 'Not just an ordinary star man; I am a RockStar!' at which we both laugh.

....

AIR FOR THY LUNGS

Another crisp December morning, the moon illuminates the sky, and casts its reflection on the ocean. The stars glitter faintly in the distant sky. The world is yet to wake up.

Ed walks towards me, greeting, 'Good morning Roy, you are early again!'.

'Ah! Yes, I have begun to love the morning quietness', I reply.

'That's good', he comments.

We walk in silence for a few minutes, before he asks me about the latest happenings at work. After relating some of the details, Ed comments on how important it is that we take time to breathe during these times of uncertainty, to eat healthy food, to drink plenty of water and to exercise so that the body and mind are in balance.

Suddenly, he asks me to name someone who had really sacrificed for me to be what I am today.

I promptly talk about my parents, my mother and my late father. I relate to him of how my mother worked two jobs, so that I could get extra tuition before my major examinations; how she sold most of her jewelry, so she could extend the house that we live in now. I reflect back to when she, despite our insistence, moved out on her own after I got married, giving away the house she built over the years with her money. I speak with pride about how she is a teacher to-date, so she could manage her monthly expenses, and how she doesn't even rely on me for medication. She always says that she has lived a fulfilling life, and that she will continue to work till she dies.

'I love these stories of parents Roy, I truly do. They inspire me beyond my imagination to realize the tenacity and the resilience of our parents. There are also people whose sacrifices go beyond the love for their families, to empower others who might be only remotely related or not know at all. Can you think of an example?', he asks.

I think for a moment and answer, 'Have you heard of Bai Fangli?'

'No, I haven't', he responds, curious to know about the example I would bring to the topic today.

I narrate from something I have seen on a social media post a couple of months earlier, 'After long years of work, Bai Fangli, a man of seventy four years retired from his pedicab driving job in some place in China. This was in 1986 if I am not mistaken'. I try to relate the story as best I can, to do justice to this humble role model.

'On his way home, he was stirred to see many children working in the field, who probably had dropped out of school due to financial difficulties. Saddened by the reality of the lack of opportunity, he decided to go back to his old job of driving pedicabs in the city to support these children's education. He first donated some 5,000 Yuan before returning to work to support them in paying their school fees,' I relate.

Ed looks impressed as I continue.

'He would often work long hours, sometimes waiting 24 hours continuously near a railway station to pick up passages at odd hours. From whatever he received, he would pay the schools with his earnings in installments', I stopped to catch my breath before continuing.

'His entire contribution for the sixteen odd years of work after his retirement summed up to three hundred and fifty thousand Yuan which is about USD fifty three thousand as per today's currency rates', I stop to reflect on what I had just said.

The coconut palms in the distance dance in the morning breeze and the crows begin to leave their nests in the wake of the dawn.

I continue, 'At the age of ninety, he paid his last installment to a school and retired from his job for the second time. In 2005, aged ninety-three, Bai died of lung cancer.'

'Wow!' Ed utters in deep respect. 'What a retirement plan! Not everyone could do that'.

'Can you see how he chose to solve a problem in the community? How he chose to empower those children?', I ask.

He nods and adds, 'It's ironic that Bai died of lung cancer; because my analogy for empowerment is in fact the lungs. It's the capacity to breathe, to create more breathing space. It's about creating the ability to absorb and take in more oxygen', Ed says.

We see the fishermen preparing their boats to return to the sea. Ed nods at them as if to acknowledge them.

He continues, 'Say you are climbing the Himalayas. There's a point when oxygen is too low and you're in a potential death zone. And if you can't adjust to this drop in the air, you die. The lung capacity supports someone to go further and further up the mountain. It's not surprising that Bai died of lung cancer, he would have breathed the fumes of gas and dust in those busy streets doing what he knew best for those children. What a sacrifice!'

I become more conscious of my breath and feel my lungs being filled with the air I breathe. We walk in silence for a while almost as if to pay our respects to Bai, our example.

'It's a beautiful organ. It's a connecting point of the body to the outside world - inhaling oxygen and exhaling carbon dioxide. Making you one with the atmosphere around you', Ed remarks.

At that moment I realize that our lives are built on the sacrifices of the previous generations, their sweat and blood, the people who were willing to let go of something they held dear to them. The people who chose to work tirelessly for us forfeiting something they may have desired, hoping that we would have a better life, a better future.

I remember a story from university. We must have walked for a while, when I decide to add further, 'One of my dearest friends from university was not very well off. So while studying, he had to find a way to support his brother and sister. He started a small mechanics workshop especially for motor bicycles. The first year was tough, and by the end of the year he was more worried about paying the meager salaries of the two mechanics and paying off the debt he owed an uncle'.

'Then one day, a middle-aged man, a distant traveler on a motorbike, stopped to check his tyres on a *Poya* day. He asked whether there was a place where he could have a cup of tea as most shops were closed on the public holiday. He mentioned that he loved motorbikes and that he would ride the countryside during the weekends and Poya days', I continue.

'My friend offered the traveler a cup of tea from the flask he had brought for himself. In the course of the conversation, when asked, my friend explained to him his story and in his desperation, he may have revealed more than he should have about his difficulties at the time. The traveler, before leaving, noted down my friend's address but did not promise anything. Around six months later, my friend received a letter from the traveler, inviting him to come see him at his office. At this point in time, my friend had already closed down his workshop as it had been more a liability than a source of income to sustain the family'.

I take a deep breath and continue again, 'It had been a small office close to Colombo, and my friend distinctly remembers ringing the bell that day wondering why he had been called there. The traveler asked my friend to sit down, and had someone bring in a cup of tea. He had smiled with my friend and said, "Nothing like a cup of tea", hinting at the moment in his last encounter when he offered him his cup of tea', I continue to relate the story.

'You are such a good story teller Roy, I am impressed', Ed says with a serious look on his face.

I laugh and continue, 'He asked my friend what became of the workshop. He asked him how much he was in debt to his uncle and handed him some money for the value he quoted. My friend was flabbergasted. It was not a lot of money at the time, but the sheer generosity swept him off his feet. He asked him whether it would be viable for him to start the business again and if he was supported at the beginning, whether he could devote some time while studying to build the workshop', I recount.

'My friend was ready to give it a try and mentioned to him a rough estimation of the resources he required. He asked my friend to think about it and come see him in a month. It was later that my friend found out who he was. He had not been a rich man himself, having started off as a clerk. Even though it was given in installments, the traveler had to save money for six months to have been able to give the total sum required for the workshop. And believe it or not, that workshop still runs in grand scale to this day. My friend who is now a mechanical engineer is also an entrepreneur who first embarked on a journey due to a dire need to look after his family. He says that it was the sacrifice that the traveler made to empower him with the resources, that created that success', I conclude.

'So inspiring Roy – you relate these stories so well!', Ed says admiringly, to which I laugh, again.

'I just need to do justice to these people who actually did the difficult work', I say in total honesty.

We walk the rest of the length in silence. Ed invites me to have *pol roti* and *roast paan* from a small *petti kade* across the railway lines. I heartily indulge myself as both Ed and I talk about our travels, pet hobbies, and children.

....

Back at work

I finally get the opportunity to speak to the managers again at a meeting. This time, the difference is that the GM and HR Director are present and they too back me up and assure the target managers that the development will continue as per their previously decided objectives, and assure me that the concerns from their one-to-ones would be addressed. They say that there had been much confusion, and that the top managers would take responsibility to make sure that it will not happen again. They reassure the group that they will not have to leave unless they really wanted to and have already decided to do so. They mention that they could now withdraw their resignation, if anyone had already submitted them.

When it was finally my turn to speak, I start by apologizing to them for having been the messenger of bad news, and for having caused distress. I apologize if I had acted in a manner that had questioned their competence or worse, affected their dignity at work and as persons overall.

Amazingly, after the meeting, I find many managers nodding away, smiling and acknowledging my apology. However, I also face displeasure from a few who choose to avoid eye contact with me.

I walk out of the auditorium, wanting to bury myself in the sand, not wanting to go back to my desk.

I hear that my boss has been asked to resign from his position, and finally I get to hear about his failed track record in the US, and how the owners of the company wanted to give him an opportunity to make it in life, given the close family relationship with the man.

Then I hear something that pleasantly surprises me, when the CEO of the cluster personally calls me and asks me to take a transfer to the 'Change and Transformation Unit' that drives change organization-wide. This is in fact a promotion, and I am simply taken aback when he says that the decision is based on my past performance and some of the feedback that they have received from the target managers themselves.

He congratulates me and says, 'Roy, we have people who are very good at what they do, absolutely brilliant in their particular job roles. But we want someone who wants to go that extra mile even in unknown territory, to make sure that they find the best solutions for the people and the organization'.

I smile in appreciation.

'And you have shown that with very little support from others. Congratulations!', he adds further in an email, confirming the offer.

While driving home that evening, I deliberately make it a point 'not to think' but to just drive and enjoy the music.

....

WOMB FOR THY CHILD

I continue to walk every morning, running whenever I can. I have not met Ed for almost two weeks now. I sometimes bring my son to the beach in his baby carrier and hold him close to my heart; this has allowed my wife to occasionally sleep for a bit longer than usual. I try my best to spend more time with my family and spend an hour or two in the week to star-gaze with my little girl. I start relating the stories my dad used to tell me about certain constellations and galaxies. This had brought a sense of calm back in to my life, a calm that reassures me that I am somehow doing what I am meant to be doing at this moment in time.

At work, I am sent on training and also I am coached by the cluster CEO himself. For the time being, I am relieved to be working from the same plant as this enables me to rebuild the strained relationships with some managers who were part of the previous initiative.

I think to myself about why I may have received conflicting information about these target managers in the focus group discussions. Like everyone else, these managers are not perfect. They try tirelessly under very stressful circumstances to meet the deadlines, and in doing so, transfer that stress on to the assembly lines. When my former boss identified this group as problematic and needing intervention, he did have a point. Even though he went about doing it the wrong way, he was right to choose these target managers as the route to create a better 'emotional environment' for the machine operators.

This realization creates a tremendous opportunity for me in my new role to really work with the managers and to equip them better to manage and regulate stress.

And that is not all. The pressure obviously comes from the layer above them. Now that is another growth opportunity.

I realize more and more that development at this stage is only sustainable if you work as growth partners; cooperating, collaborating and focusing on the win.

Much has happened in the past ten weeks. And these walks with Ed have become more and more essential in a way, to know that there is someone physically walking next to me during these tough times at work; somebody who is older, someone who hadn't had things easy.

Ed has been telling me that he would be going away for a few months. And I sincerely hope that he would continue to mentor me like this.

I ask him when I meet him this morning, what he has for me today. He laughs and says, 'From leadership to influence, influence to empowerment, and empowerment to now. Roy, this could be our last walk together'.

I look at him in surprise, 'What do you mean last walk?'

'I am going to the UK', he replies.

And before I could inquire further, Ed continues, 'You know, we've been doing this now for a number of sessions. What do you think today's session should be about?'

'I don't know, anything that you want me to know. Surely, you will be back won't you?', I ask with a sense of anxiety about his departure.

'What does it take for our impact to continue?', he asks ignoring my question. 'The type of impact that can go beyond this time and generation?'

I honestly find myself unable to answer.

'Almost like a legacy. Now what comes to your mind when you talk about legacy?', he continues to ask me.

I answer, brushing away the disappointment that I am feeling inside. 'When I think of legacy now, I think of many people. The legacy of my father and mother and many other RockStars we fail to recognize; the everyday stars in a landscape that celebrates only the glitterati, that their mere presence goes unnoticed'.

Suddenly, there is the sound of a flock of sea gulls taking off into the sky: the synchronous flapping of their wings fills the air. I turn around to see them fly upwards together, and I'm elated by the simple beauty of this sudden movement. What a beautiful backyard I have, I think to myself as someone who has always lived so close to the sea with a balcony facing the ocean.

Ed's kind voice brings me back to our conversation. 'You know, you may have noticed, in our walks, the higher we go in the topics that we speak, the less we have to talk about, because in reality we actually know very little about life'.

He continues, 'This is true – the more mature you become, the less we rely on words to convey who you are. Your identity is embedded in the ownership and action you take in what you stand for. So legacy, I believe, is completing the circle and the purpose we are born in to, creating hope for another generation'.

'Purpose?', I ask.

'Yes, what you are meant to do and fulfill', Ed replies.

We are silent for a few seconds, catching our breath and immersing ourselves in the majesty of the dawn. Lately, it looks like that Ed has wanted me to speak more while he had remained silent.

I add, 'What if we are born with a reason? One of the all-time legends of our time, Mother Theresa, fostered and nurtured many children even though she was never a biological mother. She was a loving womb to thousands of poor children in the streets of Calcutta. A real RockStar she was', I smile widely.

'What are your thoughts Ed? Am I on the right track?', I ask feeling like the one who is leading the conversation now.

'Absolutely', he responds. 'Legacy can be likened to the womb. The moment a woman gets to know that she is going to have a child, she becomes conscious of everything. She is conscious of the air she breathes, the food she eats, the places she goes to, the things she does, and so on. Everything becomes much more purposeful, because the child she is carrying becomes her purpose for those forty weeks. And at that moment, even the most careless person would want to slow down, because there's another life within her. The womb has the capacity to hold a child, to feed a child, to supply oxygen and warmth to a child', Ed narrates.

My mind drifts to the times when my wife was expecting both our children.

Ed is quiet again; this, I have begun to realize, is his way of giving me the time and the space to think and speak.

'So the idea is, may be to ask whether we can ensure this for our future generations by what we do now and today, to carry, hold, feed and provide warmth and breath for future generations. What if we have that perspective? That perspective of wanting to leave something behind for the cohorts yet to be born in places we would never be able to see in our life time?' I ask.

After a few moments of silence, he replies, 'Ultimately Roy, you need to answer some questions for yourself. I don't care how people will remember me, but I do care about what I've done for them from my end. When I close my eyes for the last time, I'd want to know that I've lived a life of purpose. A life of service. I want to be truly exhausted by having worked for the benefit of others and the betterment of society. I want to be so tired, from the way I have committed to working hard for people around me, the people who have been entrusted to me season after season', he completes.

He comments, totally engrossed in the trail of his thoughts, 'I'd like to know that I've made the circumstances better for them, and that I have helped them feel the essence of what they are meant to become'.

'I want to know that I have supported them to truly feel joy in their hearts, for ultimately, that's what we all want right? We all want happiness and fulfillment; be it through success, recognition, power, love, riches, education and achievement of our dreams', he adds.

I nod.

As if to add grandeur to our conversation, we hear a loud babble of laughter. Turning my head, I see three people – two young children and their father, running towards the beach from the shanties that line the beach side. The sound and sight of their genuine mirth and laughter, energize the entire area. I feel my spirits rising at the sight of the trio, playing and laughing near the water, despite the sun not having risen yet, despite it being so early in the morning.

'What you say sounds almost like a lifestyle – living with a purpose, living for a purpose', I add.

'Yes, a mindset shift from "me" to "we" that governs our daily decision-making', Ed says.

I nod as we walk in silence.

I bring in an example that had always intrigued me about what the world would be like if electricity was never discovered.

'You know, when Benjamin Franklin discovered electricity – he may have not known that it was capable of lighting a bulb. Edison built on Franklin's discovery. Consider what we do with electricity today. What if electricity was never discovered? Franklin is long gone, but we enjoy his work and we have built on it. Everything we boast about today, from great inventions that allow us to go to outer space, to our smart phones, depend on electricity and its' properties to mystify us with possibilities', I comment to which Ed nods his head smiling.

We walk in silence for a few more minutes, before Ed decides to stop and gaze at the horizon.

'Let's sit on that boat', he suggests, walking towards a fishing boat moored to the shore.

He seems calm and contemplative. The sky begins to turn a light blue as Venus gives way to the sun rise from the East. How spectacular it is!

'The last sight of Venus for the morning', I say smiling.

'Oh yes, see how beautifully she fades away in the sky!', Ed says as we both enjoy its transition from visible to invisible.

Ed begins after moments of indulging in the silence that we have both come to enjoy.

'This makes me think of the toughest experience I have faced as a person so far; my experience with the young mother who bled to death due to my carelessness. For years I could not forgive myself, and I kept donating blood to compensate for it till one day my son and I witnessed an accident on the road'.

'There were a few vehicles that had collided, but we both saw a motor-cyclist laying on the pavement with people beginning to gather around him. I promptly stopped the car and asked my son to wait inside before rushing to assist him. But my son, who was just five years old at the time, jumped off the car and shouted, "move, move, my dad is a doctor"', Ed recounts, smiling.

He continues, 'The motorcyclist was bleeding heavily from his arms and legs, and I noticed that his upper left arm was fractured. After trying to manage the bleeding in his other arm and legs, I realized that rushing him to the hospital would be the best thing to do. So, with the help of the bystanders, I placed him carefully in the back seat of my vehicle, and instructed my son to hold the motorcyclist's hand in a particular angle to the fracture and the bleeding'.

I fleetingly wonder at Ed's son's spunk.

Ed recalls, 'The man was screaming in pain, and my son kept telling him "My dad will heal you. He is a doctor. He will give you his blood". This repeated assurance put me in panic mode for the first time in my life. I drove so fast that day; I don't really remember how I got the person to the emergency room in the peak of traffic. My son repeatedly affirmed the person so loudly, that I had to turn around and ask him to shut up'.

Ed laughs, 'He would remain quiet for a while only to start again to console the man'.

I smile furtively, not knowing how this story would end.

Ed continues, 'Then without being able to hold it all back, I looked back and shouted at my son, "Shut up for heaven's sake Lucas, and stop talking about blood. You are only making him more nervous"'.

Ed smiles in memory. 'But the truth was that he was making ME more nervous and agitated', he admits.

'After ensuring that the guy was in the safe hands of the hospital staff we headed to the car to realize the back seat was soaked with blood. I ordered my son to sit at the front even though we normally don't permit him to do so. When I started driving again, he asked me, "Dad, aren't you going to donate your blood?"', Ed relates.

'I kept quiet', Ed says. 'He asked me again, "Dad tell me more about blood. You teach me the anatomy, the other organs in the body. What does blood do?" In frustration, I told him, "It keeps everything else alive". I really wished he would stop; and he did – for some time, before he said, with wonder in his voice, "Wow dad...like a magic potion?"'

I smile at the precociousness of Ed's story. 'What did you say, Ed?', I ask.

Ed continues his narration of the dialogue smiling. 'I told him, "Yes". "Like a cure-all?", Lucas asked again. "Yes", I repeated. "Like a secret ingredient?", he asked. "Yes", I repeated. "Like the X factor?", he asked again'.

'That did it!', Ed says. 'I said, "For goodness' sake Lucas, Stop! I am trying to drive here!"'

'Did he stop asking then?', I ask amused.

'He stopped for a while', Ed concedes. 'But then after a while, he went on to whisper in my ear, "Dad, is it like a *heart factor*? Because it starts from the heart?" I sighed loudly and told him, "Yes Lucas, it is like the heart factor and everything else you said. You were right. Now let me drive in peace!"', Ed concludes with a laugh.

Looking at me, he says 'You see, that day I spelt out, without even knowing, something very essential to myself and that is this overarching quality of blood; it is life itself. I needed to apply this heart-factor to myself to first come to terms with what happened, to let go. So Roy, the moral of this story is that ultimately it is the "heart factor" that will decide the level of maturity you grow in to. It binds everything that we discussed and life is enriched day by day because we apply this heart factor at home, work and play'.

We walk quietly again, before he comments, 'Roy, I hope you've learned something from me in the past few weeks while we were walking. I wish we had more time'.

'Ed, what are you talking about? It is just a vacation right?', my voice is laced with apprehension, doubt, and concern.

Ed smiles somewhat reassuringly, 'You see there's some good news. My colleagues in the university in the UK have asked me to start teaching and to also apply to be reinstated back to the medical profession. I am not sure whether I want to go back to practice, but I sure would like to teach'.

'Wow Ed! I'm so happy for you. I mean, wouldn't that really complete the circle for you? You should apply to be reinstated; whether you want to practice or not is entirely another story', I reply genuinely excited for him.

Ed's smile is as sanguine as ever. 'Ha! Let's see. For me Roy, these walks with you helped in some way to make meaning of my journey as a doctor'.

Ed smiles at me. As an afterthought, he adds, 'I am a bit tired Roy, the corporate world can be a ruthless place at times, I want to take it slow as I'm going to undergo a surgery after that'.

'Surgery? For what?', I demand with unease and worry.

'Well you see, my nephew is a kidney patient, and I'm a match for him. And I thought I would donate a kidney', Ed replies.

'You're kidding me, right? Your son is still ten years old!' I respond not being able to comprehend the logic behind his decision.

'No, I'm not kidding you Roy. This young man needs a kidney. He is just 22 years with an entire life before him', Ed replies calmly.

The air is still. I am completely flabbergasted and gaze at the horizon not knowing how to react to this. My heart fills with so much awe and sadness at the same time, to a point I wonder if it would burst inside me. It feels as though "my father" had said he'd give a kidney away, and the possibility that he could die, has suddenly thrown me off my feet. I don't know why I feel like this, because people can live with one kidney, right?

I realize then that even though our age difference does not qualify him to be one, I in my mind treat Ed with a sense of fatherly respect.

Struggling to find coherence, I ask, 'Can I see you in hospital or something? This is a shock!'

'No, I will be undergoing the surgery in England, because my nephew lives in England. And I will then start my teaching. Come let's walk', Ed replies jumping off the boat.

We walk for a few minutes before he stops.

He looks at me, with one of his signature looks deep yet simple, and says, 'Son, I hope that your legacy would be big enough to accommodate much more than your two children. I hope that would give you enough drive to wake up every morning with excitement. To create spheres of oxygen for many people, to a much polluted world. I am honoured to have taken this walk with you, and I will continue to be in touch with you. But for now, I will have to say goodbye. Maybe one day you will decide to visit me in England', his words are full of sincerity and warmth.

'Ed, it's been my honour. My privilege', I say – my words brimming with the emotions I feel inside.

He hugs me in a long embrace of a father and a son. Then he looks at me and winks, 'Stay blessed RockStar!'

He smiles, waves, and walks away.

'Thank you, dad', I smile and whisper under my breath flooded by an avalanche of sentiment too elusive to capture in words.

I watch him till he disappears through the line of coconut trees, and then to cross the railway tracks.

I feel a tear drop streaming down my cheek. I can't remember the last time I had tears in my eyes.

I start walking towards home myself; slow and quiet, taking my time to absorb this moment fully. There is no hurry! No hurry whatsoever!

I look back at our footprints on the sand.

From a distance, I hear the noise of the fisher-folk pulling their nets to the shore, a group of them in coordinated movements.

The landscape disappears as I begin to realize something strangely beautiful within me.

The waves sweep the shores gently and new patterns are formed on the sand.

And, then it occurs to me: maybe this completes a circle for me too.

THE END